Religious Archives: An Introduction

August R. Suelflow

Religious Archives: An Introduction

August R. Suelflow

 Society
of
American
Archivists

Chicago
1980

Library of Congress Cataloging in Publication Data

Suelflow, August Robert, 1922-
  Religious archives.

  Bibliography: p.
  1. Church archives. I. Title.
CD974.S83   25.17′14   80-17159
ISBN 0-913828-20-1

Title page: Religious archivists in 1916. Photo courtesy of the Church of Jesus Christ of Latter-day Saints.

Contents

Religious archives have grown rapidly in recent years. Above: A display area in the Mennonite Heritage Center, Winnipeg, Manitoba. Photo courtesy of the Conference of Mennonites in Canada.

Foreword

One of the most remarkable developments in the recent history of American and Canadian archival activity has been the rapid growth of religious archives. This heightened interest has been evident not only in the collection and preservation of religious records, but it has also fostered an expansion in the number of religious archival repositories. Never before have denominations, individual churches, and other religious organizations been more aware of the need for archival programs to locate their records and make them available for research use.

As an acknowledgement of the recent surge in religious archival activity, the Society of American Archivists is pleased to issue this manual. It contains chapters about the place of archives in religious organizations, collection policy, administration, acquisition, processing, reference service, and outreach programs. The manual was prepared by the Reverend August R. Suelflow, Director of Concordia Historical Institute. Over the years, the author has been a leading figure in promoting the uses of religious records and in encouraging the growth of religious archival institutions. He has also been a prolific writer on archival matters, with articles appearing in *The American Archivist* and other journals. With this manual, he has brought together many of his ideas as well as those of other prominent religious archivists into a single, comprehensive publication.

The Society deeply appreciates the cooperation and contributions of David Horn, Archives of Indiana Methodism, DePauw University; Lynn E. May, Jr., and A. Ronald Tonks, Historical Commission of the Southern Baptist Convention; William B. Miller, Presbyterian Historical Society; Earl Olson and Bill Slaughter, Historical Department, Church of Jesus Christ of Latter-day Saints; Sr. M. Felicitas Powers, Archives, Sisters of Mercy; David B. Gracy; Tom Pardo; Lawrence Klippenstein, Conference of Mennonites in Canada; Richard W. Marcus, Chicago Jewish Archives, Spertus College; and the members of the Religious Archives Professional Affinity Group. The Society is especially grateful to the National Historical Publications and Records Commission, whose support has made publication of this manual possible.

Jan Shelton Danis
Editor

Maynard J. Brichford
SAA President, 1979-80

1
The History and Nature of Religious Archives

Today there are considerably more than five hundred religious archives and historical institutions functioning at various levels. Some administer large collections, some small. Some offer an excellent range of professional services, others are no more than a closet open to the public for a few hours on an afternoon. Some have developed well-defined systems of collecting, processing, and public relations, and others seemingly still live from hand to mouth.

Diversity among religious archives is partly a legacy of collecting policies of the past. Collections frequently were accumulated by an elected church official, perhaps a secretary or clerk, who by virtue of his office happened to create or possess records. Sometimes the religious jurisdiction required maintenance of certain records. However, as the collections grew larger and their immediate practical value declined, or as one officer suceeded another, the size or geographical dispersal of such collections demanded other provisions.

Sometimes such collections of church officials were transferred to nearby church colleges or seminaries at the time of the death of the officials. Unless individual faculty members were particularly interested in them, such collections may well have been buried in closets or backrooms for many decades.

In other cases, private collectors gathered records. Such efforts may have had their roots in personal or family interests. Perhaps a professor of history was engaged in research and endeavored to collect as much as possible on a given subject. Such collections occasionally competed with those maintained by officers of the church.

Religious historical societies also contributed to the development of ecclesiastical records collections and archives. Early societies of this type were those established in the 1840s and 1850s by the Reformed Church, Presbyterians, Mormons, Lutherans, and others. All too often the group received only limited financial support from the denomination's membership, and after the first charismatic leader died, the collections fell into neglect.

In some instances, special collections were also gathered at seminary libraries, primarily because of the work or interests of professors. Very often archives and manuscript collections were considered subordinate to the theological treasures of the library. Unfortunately, some of the librarians who had responsibilities for such collections were more inclined to treat manuscripts individually as books, rather than as collections of papers emanating from an office. But at least valuable resources and documents were being gathered and preserved.

A modern observer of religious archives can detect the role once played by individual collectors, denominational officers, church history professors, historical societies, and seminary libraries. At times they worked in ignorance of one another; at other times they were in open competition; on only rare occasions did they consolidate collections or cooperate to eliminate duplication and wasted effort. Their varied approaches to records preservation has led to a boundless diversity among ecclesiastical archival collections and a wide divergence in policies and operations at religious archival agencies.

Religious archives are diverse agencies, but most collect similar types of records. Below and center right: Historian's office of the Mormon church in 1911 and the church office building, which houses the archives in 1980. Far right: Bound volumes of official records from the mid-nineteenth century. Photos courtesy of the Historical Department, Church of Jesus Christ of Latter-day Saints, and the Presbyterian Historical Society.

Collecting practices of religious archives are still diverse, but generally four basic types of agency can be identified.

- ☐ A national denominational archives that also collects considerable state or diocesan materials and even some parish records.
- ☐ A denominational archives that deals exclusively with the top administrative records of the denomination. This type does not preserve any state, diocesan, or parish records under the assumption that they are preserved on those levels. Regrettably, there if often no liaison or cooperation between such intermediate agencies.
- ☐ Active state diocesan archives within a denomination, but no denominational headquarters archives.
- ☐ The circuit or parish level, where generally little archival activity takes place.

Interestingly, a highly centralized form of church government does not necessarily produce a centralized archives but often leads to quite decentralized agencies. On the other hand, where the government of a church has been very decentralized, highly centralized archival agencies have been established.

Regardless of the type, most religious archives collect such records as minutes, correspondence, reports of their various entities, financial ledgers and reports, audit reports, records of appeals and adjudication, interoffice memos, charitable records, appointment books, registers, charters, constitutions and bylaws, legal papers, deeds, articles of incorporation, agreements, and statistical reports. The administrative level or the depth of such records will depend on the kind of archival agency the denomination has envisioned.

Some religious archives may also maintain a historical depository where all denominational journals, periodicals, convention proceedings or transactions, and other published histories and resources are collected. Still other archives may also function as museums, preserving the personal effects of some of the great leaders, worship resources, clerical apparel, altars, pulpits, lecterns, and communion vessels.

The best acquisition and preservation principles and policies count for naught unless the collections are consulted. Consequently religious archivists must address themselves to the services rendered by archives. Here is a brief list of the various types.

- ☐ Provide reference and research services.
- ☐ Supply and provide access to photographic and photoduplication services.
- ☐ Participate in educational programs, especially publications and exhibits.
- ☐ Render counsel in the preparation of parish histories, anniversary services, and other special events.
- ☐ Offer suggestions for the accurate maintenance of church records and their safekeeping.
- ☐ Offer lectures, particularly on historical and archival subjects.
- ☐ Conduct historical tours, place historical markers, and maintain historical shrines.

As a general rule, it is inadvisable to start a service unless it can be continued. Priorities in the type and nature of the services rendered should be considered. It is unwise at all times to say no to a request of an official regardless of how busy one is or how thoroughly buried the information may seem. This is the bread and butter service. On the other hand, one must be less generous in rendering services if the

demands exceed the capacity of an overburdened staff. Consideration might be given to the greater utilization of volunteer workers in providing the kinds of services that clients desire.

This manual makes general suggestions in several areas. Some issues seem particularly important, especially defining an appropriate scope of collection and establishing procedures, including records management, for the orderly acquisition of suitable material. Also addressed are staff training, budgets, processing, and reference service. Each religious archives must make its own translation of these general suggestions into specific policies and practices consistent with its type, stage of development, programs, and mission. Finally, archivists of religious depositories are especially urged to serve their constituency with commitment and efficiency. This may be their finest and most effective tool for sustaining their archives.

2
The Place of Archives in Religious Organizations

The management and support of religious archives frequently vary as much as their objectives, scope, and activities. Some depositories remain in the unenviable position of serving as adjuncts to theological libraries, to officers, or to boards uninterested in archives. Others are fortunate enough to be directed by full-time executives with adequate staffs supported by policy-making boards responsible to denomination conventions or assemblies.

Religious archival depositories have frequently been established as private ventures and have often remained just that. Sometimes, in the absence of archival leadership or policy, a theological seminary library, educational institution, or even a secular university has collected denominational resources. Sometimes unofficial efforts to preserve valuable documents and artifacts have zealously been supplied by a historical society. On other occasions state or municipal agencies or libraries have served as depositories for ecclesiastical records because of competence and proximity. None of these arrangements best meets the needs of a religious archives. The most effective archives program in a church is one properly authorized and maintained by the parent denomination or geographical unit that creates the records. Cooperative ventures between several agencies in a communion should not be ruled out. For such a merged agency, relationships and responsibilities between sponsors — whether secular or church — must be spelled out to eliminate operational and legal confusion, and the possibility of dissolution of the arrangement must be allowed. A denomination or religious organization establishing an archives must create specific resolutions and statutes (canon law). Ideally, these should be drafted and adopted by the highest legislative authority, such as the top-level convention, the house of bishops, the conference of presidents, or, where applicable, the top official. In other words, the establishment, authorization, and provision for a denomination archival agency should come from the highest level rather than from an intermediate or subordinate one. Also, an archives should be established formally, not organized by mere interoffice memorandum.

For most effective results, policy statements should be embodied in the constitution or code book of the church or religious entity itself. The formulation may be brief and simple, but it must be precise and clear. The formulation should identify the general collecting policies, describe the scope of the collection, provide for an orderly and routine transfer of records from administrative and board offices, and contain adequate references to personnel and control. Specifically, also, ownership — whether retained by the authorizing agent or by the archives — should be spelled out. An archives can be enabled to carry out all activities and functions of a legal corporation.

The administrative relationships and responsibilities to the communion or denomination itself need to be fully defined. Ideally, the archival agency should be governed by a separate policy-making board, on which the highest level decision-makers serve or are represented.

Policy statements should also clearly identify financial support, budgetary provisions, and the like. Far too often, church archives initiated by a private undertaking or by a historical society have been inadequately and haphazardly supported. Archival budgets must come from the church budget itself, assuring the kind of continuity essential to its ongoing programs. Although society membership dues and contributions from "angels" can augment budgets, they should never be expected to finance most of a church archives program. Allocate such funds for special projects and do not use them for operating expenses.

Avenues of communication, transfer, replevin, and acquisition need to be spelled out. Much can be accomplished when the church, in its canon or ecclesiastical policy formulations, carefully defines what is to be done with the records and files created by its offices. The board or the church authority responsible for such formulations ought to define the collecting authority, maintenance, and service responsibilities of the archival agency with respect to the records-creating offices. A general statement such as the following should be adopted by every top level policy-formulating board:

> The (here specify the offices, executives, boards, and committees) shall transfer correspondence, records, and other papers from their respective offices to the archives ten years after creation or when they are no longer of current operational value for the purpose of preserving these materials and making them available for research.

Avenues of communication between church and archives should be spelled out. Above: The chairman of the history-archives committee and the historian-archivist examine records together. Photo courtesy of the Mennonite Heritage Center, Conference of Mennonites in Canada.

Specific directives should apply to the transfer of records of temporary committees, member congregations, secretaries of various conferences and assemblies, auxiliary organizations, institutions and other agencies within the church. Good records management will provide for the automatic transfer of records from the creating office to the archives.

The archives department or commission should be given the responsibility to see that all the records created by the church ultimately come under inventory control, endowing the archivist with the final authority to determine whether records are created that adequately document the functions and programs of the church.

3
Defining the Scope of the Collection

All too frequently religious archives function without clear objectives, without a thoroughly and adequately defined scope of the collection. Newly established archival agencies may be tempted to be too inclusive in the collecting program. This error is based on the assumption that the depository can earn more respectability by reporting huge quantities of materials than by emphasizing limited, narrowly defined, intensely valuable collections. The archivist who regularly pleads "send me everything you have" is building an ecclesiastical attic. Too many potential donors may feel, because of family or personal pride, that their papers and possessions belong in a public institution. This problem becomes very serious when materials of questionable value are received with an obligation to preserve them in perpetuity.

Operating without a clear scope of the collection results in a hodgepodge of resources and often the neglect of the substantive records created in the administrative offices of the church. As a general principle, the scope of the collection of any religious records depository should be neither too broad or too narrow, but it should be oriented primarily to the group that it serves. The sponsoring organization, which underwrites the cost, has the right to expect the archives to meet the needs of the denomination. This should be the first factor considered in defining a scope of collection.

A religious body or organization has the obligation to preserve those records and resources necessary to continue its operations, to meet its legal

A religious archives preserves those records that provide for its historical continuity and that promote
understanding of its operations and objectives.
Above: Letters of Luther Rice, a founder of Baptist
mission work in America, are displayed with a
historic gavel. Top right: Modern microfilm is jux-
taposed with an antique ledger. Photos courtesy of
the Historical Commission of the Southern Baptist
Convention. Bottom right: Cartographic aids are
used to determine the location of church records and
to assist researchers in congregational and family
history. Map showing boundaries of districts and
conferences of Indiana Methodism in 1852. Drawn
by Barbara F. Poor, courtesy of the Archives of Indiana United Methodism, DePauw University.

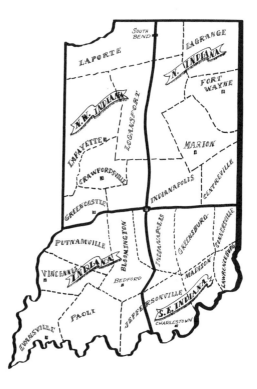

requirements, and to provide for its historical continuity. Thus, if the purposes of the organization are broad the scope of the collections of the archives will be equally broad; if narrow, they will naturally be that.

Second, the scope must include all things that will help the administrator, the executives, the religious leaders, the visitors, and the scholars understand any phase of the history, operations, goals, and objectives of the ecclesiastical body. This consideration makes a three-fold approach to historical preservation as provided by an archives-library-museum combination ideal for American churches today.

The term "archives" may be legitimately used in a broad sense, and most archival depositories, religious and nonreligious, include published literature and artifacts. The manner in which information is recorded does not make it more or less desirable for historical documentation, nor is the medium of recorded history exclusively manuscript, printed, mimeographed, photoduplicated, or any other type of writing. The artist's conception, the hastily drawn sketches of an eye witness, articles of clothing, personal effects, oral and visual resources, and museum artifacts all help the patrons understand the context and environment in which decisions were made and services performed. Let them hear the music, look at the photographs, watch film clips and videotape, read the reports, scan the letters, and, if it were possible, even sniff the midnight oil. A vital task of a department or commission on archives and history is to teach, and all the human senses should be enlisted in the learning process. This guards the collecting policy from the too subjective criteria of a single individual.

A third aspect of defining the scope of the collection is the development of an instrument by which the archives automatically receives records from administrative offices so that the archivist need not beg and argue for every transfer of material. Records management, archives committees, and disposition schedules are discussed in more detail in Section 5. The purpose of a well-defined collection policy is to protect the archives from a deluge of unwanted paper and an obligation to preserve it all. More recent records, especially, need not necessarily be retained in their entirety. Some archival agencies, for example, will collect anything produced before the 1860s but will be much more selective about material created thereafter. A well-defined collection policy will at the same time help protect the archives from the dearth of valuable resources that would result if poor records management diverted records temporarily or permanently.

The archival program should establish, through the definition of its scope, ground rules on preservation or destruction, acquisition, processing, and servicing. For this reason an archival-historical agency should be separately incorporated; property ownership is involved. The parameters of collecting and transmitting of resources will determine the strength and status of the department of archives and its role of service in the overall program of the church.

Considerations that should not determine the scope of the collection include today's levels of space, staff, and funds, although these relative factors often influence collecting policy. Thoroughness in historic documentation should not be sacrificed to insufficient facilities and financial resources; improvements should be inaugurated as soon as possible. Neither should an archives embark on an unnecessarily broad collecting program if, by some miracle, there is a surfeit of space and money. Personality likewise must not prejudice the scope of the collection — neither the archivist's powers of persuasion nor the charisma of a religious leader. Rather the permanently valuable records of the church, including its subdivisions, subsidiaries, and affiliates, regardless of its far-flung activities over vast geographical areas, should be identified because they are the "stuff" that constitute its historical resources.

Finally, the collecting policy will also be influenced by the resources collected and available at other depositories, so that competition and duplication can be avoided. Nothing will do more to avoid misunderstanding and competition than to spell out the scope of the collections. This is so important but too frequently overlooked.

What, then, might a religious archives contain? The following brief checklist is offered as a suggestion for beginning to define a scope of collection.

☐ Reports of conventions and conferences, official minutes of boards and commissions, committee reports, mission reports, and financial and legal records produced by the officers and staff of the religious agencies served.

☐ Manuscripts, especially the correspondence of the members and leaders of the church, sermons, special reports and observations, journals, and diaries.

☐ Church books, whether published or in manuscript. The agenda, liturgies, formularies, catechisms, hymnals, instruction manuals, Bibles, and prayer books produced by the

denomination should be collected.

☐ Periodicals and other resources issued by the denomination or its subunits.

☐ Maps and photographs used or issued by the workers in the denomination.

☐ Parish or congregational records and historical materials, including records of membership, baptisms, and marriages, as well as general church histories, published histories, and other materials that relate the story of a local congregation in its environment.

☐ Biographical sketches of professional workers such as clergymen, teachers, and lay leaders of the denomination; these may be either in printed or manuscript form.

☐ Commemorative medallions, coins, and medals and artifacts or museum pieces such as paraphernalia used by traveling missionaries, communion vessels, altar furnishings, and other church-related items.

4
Basic Requirements

Budgets and Support
The cost of any program, especially archives-history work, is dependent upon the objectives, purposes, responsibilities, and assignments given to it. Most unfortunately, a great number of excellent archival agencies among the American churches have at times been established on the backs of dedicated and consecrated administrators. Far too often, a limited archives, like the ancient Hebrews in Egypt, have been expected to produce bricks without straw. This situation sometimes results when a charismatic leader, an interested church history professor, or someone in a similar capacity took it upon himself single-handedly to provide archives services. For this reason let it be said most emphatically that a good archives program can be established only after its authority and scope have been defined. The financial or budgetary matters then follow more easily.

Insufficient funds are detrimental to the establishment and operations of basic archival programs. The vast majority of the weaknesses, problems, and negative aspects in a denominational archival program are invariably due to a pitifully inadequate budget. When scarcity prevails, one usually finds some of the following problems:

- [ ] A willingness to accept substandard goals and objectives
- [ ] An over-burdened and inadequate staff
- [ ] Congested facilities and limited and outmoded equipment
- [ ] A retarded acquisition program
- [ ] Undesirable relationships with church authorities and administrators, often degenerating into a politicking, pleading archivist
- [ ] Failure to render reference and research services.

Such a damaged archival program constitutes a vicious circle leading to further shrinking budgets. What, then, is needed? Two basic principles of archival budgeting procedures are essential but seldom exercised: the budget of the department must be prepared by the agency itself, and the agency itself must have the opportunity to defend its budget before those who set it.

In budget preparation, the archival agency must be assured of continuity and continuous support. To accomplish this, it needs to make plans with short- and long-range goals. No budgeting can succeed without this.

Foundation grants, endowments, gifts, and bequests all should be actively sought. Where individuals and corporations may be prevailed upon to endow a research position or to supply the funds for manuscript processing and the like, these should be solicited; but again, as in the case of membership income, such funds should be allocated only for extra-budgetary items. An archival agency should also give serious consideration to making service charges in areas that are above and beyond the call of duty, as defined in the authority and scope, if the operating budget is incapable of carrying these services and courtesies. Before implementing service charges, however, it would be well to ask how such charges would affect the public image of the institution, and to ask how complete the finding aids and resources of the institution are. Scrupulously avoid imposing charges on members and officers of the church who already actively support the archival program.

Naturally, the funding of the archives department will to a great extent be dependent upon the rapport established with the church's budget makers and the ongoing public relations program conducted by its staff. A vigorous information program can go a long way toward raising both the prestige and the usefulness of the institution and its personnel. The host of techniques of public relations include the ubiquitous press release, bulletin services, newsletters, the development of finding and retrieval aids, prompt and expeditious answering of mail, rendering unique services, and the like. These are discussed in Section 10.

In summary, there is no substitute for official church support of the archives department even if society memberships, gifts, grants, and endowments are available. The church budget must provide for all its archives and history needs in a continuing, ongoing manner. Today's churches require studies in self-understanding and criticism so they can plan meaningfully for the future. Financing their own archives will go far in enabling them to do just that. The "hot stove league" of lobbyists, independent amateurs, and idly curious must give way to the sound archival-historical functions and services financed by the churches.

Buildings and Facilities

Years ago a basement, a closet, or an attic might have served as a depository for an archives collection, but soon the musty darkness encouraged mildew and attracted vermin, or dry heat produced brittleness and ashes. Even today some poorly planned denominational archival agencies do not provide adequate security or temperature and humidity controls. This has happened when abandoned rooms or other surplus facilities are made available, which had not been built to house archival-historical resources.

Adequate buildings and facilities are extremely necessary. Strive only for the best when you have the opportunity. All too frequently the ignorant assume that any place is good enough to house old papers and documents. Decades later, when the records have deteriorated badly because of poor atmospheric conditions, mishandling, improper filing, roaches, silverfish, and termites, regrets will not restore them.

The buildings and facilities of archival agencies must provide the internal and external security necessary to preserve the integrity of the collections. There should be adequate space for processing materials, displays and exhibits, reference and research services, and photoduplication service. Such facilities ought to provide maximum protection, efficient use of space, easy access to resources, and areas for group meetings and conferences. Ideally the building should be designed for separate routing of visitors and researchers. Such a separation aids in security as well as providing a quiet study area for those engaged in research.

Suitable buildings and equipment are essential. This page: Congregational records stored in a janitor's closet present a dismal contrast to the modern facility of the Concordia Historical Institute, Lutheran Church—Missouri Synod. Next page: Archives boxes, records-center type cartons, adjustable steel shelving, and a temperature and humidity monitor are part of well-equiped stacks. Photos courtesy of the Department of Archives and History, Concordia Historical Institute; the Archives of Indiana United Methodism, DePauw University; the Presbyterian Historical Society; and the Archives, Sisters of Mercy of the Union.

It is better to sacrifice convenience and centrality of location for good, well-appointed, functional, and adequate buildings and facilities. Records centers have proven that physical association with the creating offices or the headquarters agencies is not absolutely essential. Nevertheless the creating agencies and the archives should be in close proximity wherever possible. The location of the archives may easily influence the contents of the collection. If the creating offices are too distant from the archives, the latter may receive very little. Under such circumstances the archives may collect outside of its parameters simply because space is available. The archives should not be too far off the beaten path, because then accessibility and usefulness will certainly decline. Service to the executives of the church body must be borne in mind. "Out of sight, out mind," is also true with respect to archives. If administrators do not have opportunities and occasions to visit, to seek, and to inquire, they may be less inclined to use and to budget. Generally, centrality, transportation facilities, and proximity to a denominational seminary and headquarters are all extremely important.

What about the arrangements of the storage facility? Versatile, adjustable shelving of the type produced by the Library Bureau are the most practical. In the majority of religious archives, the collections consist of maps, microfilm, books, periodicals, pamphlets, papers, manuscripts, correspondence, documents, photographic slides, minutes, and other records. The width, height, and weight of such materials vary greatly. Open shelving is easier and cheaper to maintain than cabinet filing; and since the size and volume of materials cannot be predetermined, it will be most useful and practical to store as little as possible in filing cabinets and the maximum in boxes and on shelves. Filing boxes, both the Hollinger and Magafile type or the large Paige boxes, can be handled easily. In fact, it is entirely conceivable that an archives could operate beautifully without a single filing cabinet. Boxes together with adjustable steel shelving will not hamper the archivist by any rigidity of form or function. Savings in money and space can then be used to the greatest possible advantage.

Temperature and humidity control is essential, particularly in areas of the country where great fluctuations prevail. Not only archival materials, but movies, filmstrips, microfilm, and similar resources can best be preserved when the temperature remains below 70 degrees Fahrenheit and the humidity at 50 percent. Fluctuations in either cause grave deterioration and will not assure preservation in the future.

Every possible protection against fire should be provided. The question is still being debated whether an archives should be equipped with a sprinkler system or carbon dioxide or chemical extinguishers. Since papers saturated with water may be as irretrievably damaged as those charred by fire, many authorities feel chemical systems are superior.

The archives must also take precautions to protect records against theft and damage. Not even an executive should be granted the privilege of rifling through collections after they have been transferred to the archives. Complete and accurate information should be maintained recording names, dates, and addresses of all who used the resources. To be sorry after a loss has occurred provides neither comfort nor restoration of the document. Section 7 on reference service further discusses the use of collections. Timothy Walch's *Archives and Manuscripts: Security*, a volume of the Basic Manual Series published by the Society of American Archivists, contains excellent, practical advice on these topics.

Personnel and Staff

The ideal church archivist is a trained professional, equally at home in the techniques and methodology of archival administration and in the ecclesiastical history of the denomination or agency that she serves. A historian might develop into a good archivist, but merely because she happens to be a historian in no way automatically qualifies her as an archivist. If a choice must be made, begin with a professionally trained archivist who will subsequently acquire the necessary background in church history. While an archivist must be a historian, a historian need not be an archivist in order to be successful. Much more could be said, but in brief the head of the agency should have professional training and competence in archives administration and ecclesiastical history.

Of course, there are other choices if no professionally trained archivist is available. The denomination might engage a professor of American history, or a zealous amateur, or a retired executive, or a person trained in library science. But frankly, all such church backgrounds are only the beginning. Training in archives administration is essential.

Various kinds of special training are available to the archivist serving a religious depository through courses that are offered at several universities. Those of the American University, the University of Denver, and the University of Illinois are among the best known, but a host of others are also available. Membership in national and regional professional societies, extensive use of their journals, and participation in conferences and workshops all are of great advantage. Valuable information can be obtained at the annual meetings of the Society of American Archivists and through its journal, *The American Archivist*.

Some of the American communions also conduct special conferences. The oldest, since 1945, is the Conference on Archives and History, conducted biennially by the Concordia Historical Institute, St. Louis, Missouri. Many additional publications, conferences, internships, and institutes of various types are regularly offered. For more information, write to the Society of American Archivists.

The demands made upon a religious archivist are intensely specialized and yet extremely broad, almost always requiring personal sacrifices and dedication. Ernst Posner refers to the head of a department of archives and history as a "homo universalis," which implies that he ought to be "all things to all men." Besides being a historical scholar, the archivist must be both a specialist and a generalist with a talent for administration and a friend of lawmakers and patriotic societies and genealogists; he must be concerned with good public relations, equipped with common sense, dedicated to serve, and many other things.

Generally the religious archivist ought to possess the following qualifications:

☐ Physical, mental, and emotional health and vigor
☐ The gifts, qualities, interest and knowledge necessary for scholarly research into the history of the church and religious historiography
☐ A thorough understanding of archival techniques and methodology
☐ An ability and competence in working with supervisory boards, peer executives, and public relations
☐ An ability to communicate and interpret the history of the church, including an acquaintance with exhibit and display techniques
☐ A basic knowledge of library science
☐ An ability to evaluate and appraise historical resources for preservation or destruction
☐ A willingness to continue professional growth
☐ An ability to counsel and advise researchers in the utilization of historical resources and employees in archival techniques and methodology
☐ An intelligent understanding and appreciation of the purposes, objectives, and means at the disposal of the church.

Because the work of a religious archivist is professional, specialized, and demanding, the financial compensation ought to be commensurate. Unfortunately, it usually is not. The requirement makes it quite difficult for the average denomination to find someone qualified. The person in charge of religious archives is a hybrid, who crosses the lines between the academician and the traditional church executive. Salary schedules should not be based, as they often are, on the number of people working in the department, or on the basis of the total financial allotment made to the archives in comparison to other departments. The invaluable and irretrievable collections entrusted to the archivist's care must be considered in the salary evaluations. In this respect, the archivist is like a bank president, responsible for treasures that simply cannot be replaced in the event of loss or deterioration. In contrast to the librarian, most of whose resources are replaceable, the archivist has custody of unique items that are far more precious even than gold on an escalating market. Although human and financial resources may be replenished, the historical resources in an archives cannot.

As the religious archivist gains greater proficiency and specialization in her task, her general capabilities for other church-related functions diminish. As a result, there may be very few openings within the denomination for her, which might cause feelings of frustration. She may come to be viewed by her superiors as indispensable, thus limiting her chances for advancement in other areas of service. Perhaps this is not a problem to the dedicated church archivist who has no intention of shifting positions, but it may contribute to the difficulty in attracting younger workers into the field.

Most church archivists are intensely interested in conducting research and writing of their own. However, because they are frequently overburdened with responsibilities, they more often are like a midwife who has assisted in the birth of countless articles and books but has never produced an offspring of her own. This requires dedication — perhaps consecration is a better word!

Something also needs to be said about the status of the church archivist in the denomination and in the general structure of the ecclesiastical order. Since the professionalization of the office is comparatively recent — and there still may not be more than a dozen in the entire country who devote their full time to such work — the archivist may appear to stand on the outside rather than on the inside of the structure. Far too often the attitude of religious organizations faced with century-old tasks, has been that the archives are little more than the icing on the cake of church objectives.

In many denominations there is an amazing lack of consciousness of the professional standards required of a church archivist, all too frequently showing itself in the deplorable lack of understanding of the staff budget needs. The archivist is dependent upon church legislation and financial provisions, and yet the very individuals and groups who are forced to make such allocations have, at best, only a passing acquaintance with the demands of the work. Education of church executives in this respect is a vital task of the archivist.

5
Acquisition of Archival Materials

Are special acquisition programs and policies really essential for an official agency? Obviously, if the flow of all necessary materials past and present were automatic and continuous, the answer would be "no." However, all archives have one thing in common; normally there is nothing automatic and continuous about the transmission of resources to depositories. Why not?

In some cases, of course, the transmission route from creating agency or office to the archives has never been formally outlined. Even when it has, there are instances where offices forever feel that they need constant and immediate access to the records that they have created. This remains true in spite of the fact that in business, records are considered active only as long as they require a minimum of four references per file drawer per month; in the federal government, one reference per cubic foot of material per month is the criterion for active records.

Church executives and administrators, like some of their counterparts in government, business, and universities, may feel that confidential information in their files must remain under their personal custody. They fail to realize how frequently, after death, members of the family or successors in office go through papers and destroy voluminous files because of ignorance. Far better had a professional archivist or a records manager appraised them.

Fear of losing access to the records and reluctance to relinquish control of the information in them are the two attitudes that most commonly impede an orderly transfer and acquisition program.

Such reactions may be due to the lack of confidence that the records creator has in the archival agency or its staff. Do such executives fear that as soon as their records are transmitted to the archives, they become public property, to which anyone, even their most awesome enemies, may have immediate access? Do they fear their work will not bear scrutiny? Does modesty cause them to think their records are not significant enough to merit preservation? In the majority of cases, undoubtedly, they harbor a suspicion that records sent to the archives may no longer be retrievable or perhaps even identifiable, an understandable fear if they become homogenized with the accumulation and clutter in a poorly operated archives.

It is the task of religious archivists to ensure that false images do not lead records creators to hesitate or neglect to transfer materials to the archives. They must abandon haphazard systems of seeking papers and files if valuable acquisitions do not actually follow. They cannot wait until the eleventh hour or even the twelfth, when it is too late to seek records without proper educational programs and transmission machinery. They must not accept a deluge of unappraised material. They should be careful that limitations of space, staff, finances, or even geographical separation from headquarters do not cause interruptions in the orderly and continuing flow of materials.

Techniques for Locating Materials

There are many techniques and methods of locating suitable resources to be added to the historical collection. The following list is not intended to be exhaustive.

□ Develop instruments and agreements that make it canon or statutory law that all records-creating agencies, offices, and executives of the religious body apply on a continuous and regular basis specific retention and destruction policies. Official materials slated for preservation should automatically flow into the archives without nagging and cajoling from the archivist.

□ Apply, as a professional archivist, proper and necessary safeguards in destroying or retaining records. Remember that "to dispose in perfect order is the prerogative of God alone," but in the meantime establish a good acquisition program to function on sound appraisal standards. See Maynard J. Brichford's *Archives and Manuscripts: Appraisal and Accessioning,* a volume in the Basic Manual Series published by the Society of American Archivists.

- Never allow limitations of space or staff to dictate policies in your acquisition programs. Neither should a geographical separation from the headquarters by itself determine destruction and retention issues.
- Prepare check lists and inventories to ascertain whether the records in the archives are complete or whether certain elements are still missing. Abandon hasty, frantic, and sporadic spurts of effort in collecting programs. The check list should contain references to potential resources: manuscripts, documents, reports, pictures, correspondence, and other materials. With this and an inventory of what is already contained in the depository, the locator can check for specifics and can stop making broadside appeals, which, like buckshot, are fired endlessly into flocks of ducks without ever bringing one down.
- Be a detective. Know the facts in the case — that is, the history of the situation, the specific resources relating to it, and the people (even their descendants) who may have been involved. Without this knowledge, the locating job will be difficult.
- Utilize the services of a network of collectors, regional assistants, and local search parties. In a national denomination these could be the "state archivists" or "local chapters" or even individual friends and patrons. The staff of a national or international denominational agency cannot keep eyes and ears open for local materials as they turn up in attics, basements, and unexpected and unpublicized places. Religious archival agencies could also make arrangements for such assistance in retrieving resources missed in a former generation.
- Acknowledge every receipt of archival and manuscript resources. Each item, whether relatively unimportant or highly significant, should be acknowledged in writing. To ignore contributions suggests not only ingratitude but, what is worse, incompetence. Besides, a donor with a huge cache of materials at her disposal may have merely transmitted a sampling to explore the archivist's reaction. A warm, personal letter of thanks may smooth the way for the acquisition of additional resources. This is only good common sense and courtesy.
- Constantly work at establishing confidence and building trust, not only with the records-creating agencies but also with the ecclesiastical administrators and their descendants. Allay misgivings and fears especially when personal diaries, papers, and correspondence may be forthcoming. A simple way to overcome reluctance is to invite frequent inspection and to maintain an ongoing educational program. If necessary, potential donors can be assured that while most materials are generally open to the public, the most sensitive items might be closed for a specified period of time or made available only under some form of restricted access.
- Develop a budget that includes funds for rehabilitation and restoration. An archival collection treated with professional restoration techniques such as encapsulation or lamination and housed under ideal atmospheric conditions inspires confidence and promotes donations.
- Be immutably dedicated to the principle of service and research so that religious archives do not merely become warehouses or deep freeze storage lockers. Religious archivists ought to be engaged in an ongoing service and research program, and not be satisfied by merely receiving and inventorying what has been deposited.
- Practice good public relations. Specifically, the archivist who regularly reports receipts in news stories, requests people to be on the alert for certain documents, and generally keeps his clientele informed, will find that cooperation will be intensified. Make the most of regional and jurisdictional conventions (preferably with a personal appearance and displays), conferences of professional organizations, national and regional newspapers, and the like.
- Acquire adequate budgets for the archival agency to attain objectives outlined, including special funds for travel, communications, appraisals, and research.
- Do not overlook mutual and reciprocal exchanges and consultations. If items are offered that do not fall within the scope of your collections, these ought to be made available to another depository where they do belong. Much good can come of a give-and-take relationship with other denominational archives, theological seminaries, state historical agencies, and similar groups. State and local historical organizations may attempt to compete with regional religious depositories. Some state archives, for example, assume that the records of any defunct religious organization are fair game. Since these are public institutions, the public archives maintains the right to collect them. Competition, of course, does not solve the problem. A working agreement between secular and religious depositories must and can be developed, especially when materials are available in multi-copies.

Records Management and Appraisal

Denominational offices are paper producers and users in the same manner as insurance companies or government agencies. With the application of ever newer duplication devices, the volume of paper created in an average church headquarters is often of staggering proportions. The increasing amounts of paper make it neither prudent nor possible for the archives simply to serve as a storage center for outdated and unwanted correspondence, records, and office files. Naturally, records management problems are not peculiar to religious institutions, but general principles often can be applied to many different organizations.

Two particular dangers face the larger denominations as they awake to the necessity of preserving what is vital and destroying the trivia: that every shred of paper, memo, and correspondence file is turned over to the archives, or that the archives receives no office files of value because they have all been destroyed by a high-powered records officer in the denominational headquarters. Neither of these two extremes represents the kind of records management that the denominations require nor adequately preserves the important historical, legal, and ongoing records of a denomination. A balance is essential.

An institution requires both records management and archives administration. Basically, distinctions may be made between the two functions: records management is the proper care, handling, and service of current, operational records; archives management involves the proper care, preservation, and service of noncurrent, nonoperational records of historical or legal value. While it is possible to conceive of these two phases of record-keeping as a single operation, in practice it is better to maintain records management services under the archives authority.

By developing a records management program for the denominational headquarters, religious archives often can produce lasting benefits and ongoing services to the church. The concern of the archives with the day-to-day accumulation of working records created by the agencies, boards, and commissions of a church body leads to these advantages for the denomination:

☐ Assures that all current and operational records required for the ordinary functions of the office are retained as necessary. Such records may also have legal, historical, or archival value.

☐ Alleviates the problem of adequate storage in departmental offices, saves space, and reduces

20

Good scheduling assures the systematic transfer of noncurrent records from office files to the archives. Administrative secretary, archives assistant, and archivist are key steps in this important process. Photos courtesy of the Archives, Sisters of Mercy of the Union.

costs of acquiring and maintaining filing equipment;

□ Provides administrative requirements for unified, coordinated management of files, saves time and effort, and accomodates every efficiency an expert seeks;

□ Identifies records of permanent value and provides for their perpetuity while protecting the archives from an obligation to store unwanted departmental records;

□ Preserves the principle that the religious entity itself has a logical and final interest in the records created by its agencies.

Good records management also produces benefits for the religious archives in its concern for the preservation of records. Participation in records management is decision making about the ultimate destruction or retention of materials. It establishes the effective and continuing flow into the archives of all records that have archival and historical value and safeguards the interests of the depository from being coerced into accepting unimportant records.

Good records management is best conducted with retention and disposal schedules to be applied by the staff periodically, at the end of the year or other practical and convenient unit of time. Such schedules provide the timetable for the routine transfer of noncurrent records out of office areas, for the appropriate destruction of records, and for the orderly flow of suitable records into the archives.

The schedules should be set up by the archivist in consultation with the makers and users of the records. Schedules for the retention or destruction of denominational records are best developed directly from proven organizational needs for documentation. Schedules used elsewhere may prove to be inadequate when applied to a religious body. Specific decisions should be based on the record inventories and recommendations made by executives, records officers, boards, and committees. Final authority, however, must be vested with the archivist.

In establishing and implementing retention and destruction schedules, the archivist should have the advice and support of a special records committee. The committee should consist of a convenient number of top-level executives and heads of departments of the denomination (the staff and line officers of the church), legal counsel, a church historian, and the chief of the archival-historical agency. The existence of the records committee guarantees that the judgment of persons with a broad perspective of denominational goals is directed toward the preservation of records.

The archivist evaluating or appraising any accumulation of records will be seeking satisfactory answers to several questions: What records may be destroyed immediately? What records may be destroyed later? When may that destruction be done properly? What records must be kept indefinitely? Generally speaking, it is better to designate records as having "indefinite" rather than "permanent" value. The latter term implies unalterable and forever. "Indefinite" suggests that a reappraisal may be made at some future date; this may be quite essential.

Sometimes it's a bit difficult to decide at the time a record is created whether it will have permanent or ongoing value. Such decisions can often be made more effectively in retrospect, rather than prospect. However, when the instrumentality or the mechanics for such decisions have been prepared on the basis of sound records retention and destruction schedules, both the records management phase and the archival-historical phase will be eased. Each religious body must tailor its program to its own specific contemporary and future needs.

It simply will not work to save everything. Nor will it work to destroy everything. The higher the level of operation in an agency, the greater the amount of material that must be saved. The lower the level of operation, the less that need be saved.

In determining the value of records, apply these questions to the files:

☐ Do the records have evidential value and contain unique information, that is, data that can be found only in your files and not elsewhere? If the evidence or information is found exclusively in your files, save the records.

☐ Do the files contain any materials that really do not pertain to your activity but were used only for comparison and reference? Such records may be destroyed.

☐ Are the records and files credible, authentic, and accurate? If not, the records may be destroyed.

☐ Are the files understandable or meaningful? A unique shorthand system, for example, may be legible to the writer only. Do you have files and resources that are comprehensible to you and incomprehensible to other people? Computer records sometimes fall into this category. Unless records can be understood and are meaningful to others, and unless the hardware will be available to read computer records in the future, there obviously is little sense in retaining such resouces. To be preserved, records must be meaningful and understandable.

☐ Will the records be accessible to researchers in the future? There is little point in preserving records that cannot be used.

☐ Will the records that you are preserving serve any basic purpose in the next generation? Will the files be required for future references? Again, if the answer is no, the records may be destroyed.

☐ What relationships do your records have to other existing records? The answer to this question may also help decide whether such resources should be retained or destroyed.

It is far better to begin a program of retention and destruction before a warehouse of records suddenly must be evaluated and disposed of. Procedural programs that can be applied continuously and regularly should be developed. Just as "not all which glitters is gold" so also not all scraps of paper have historical value. They must be assayed by professionals to prohibit deluging the office or archives on one hand or, on the other, irretrievably destroying the evidence that a growing and expanding church must consult in order to plan meaningfully for the future.

Oral History

The archivist may find oral history interviews with contemporary and superannuated leaders in the denomination helpful if written records must be supplemented. The subject should be notified well in advance and given an opportunity to reflect on the outline of subjects that are to be discussed. The interviewer should be knowledgeable about the subjects covered, tactful, and skillful in directing the conversation.

Transcribe the taped interview as soon as possible. There may be some sounds and gurgles that will not be easily understandable; foreign terms, proper nouns, and infrequently used words also may cause some difficulty at times. Consequently, it is advisable to send the transcript to the person who was interviewed to permit corrections, elaborations, and emendations. At that time the interviewee may also authenticate the transcribed document by signing it. Much assistance can be received from the Oral History Association, North Texas State University, P.O. Box 13734, NTSU Station, Denton, Texas 76203.

6
Processing Archival Materials

Receiving

After an item has been located and acquired for the depository, it must be carefully handled in a variety of ways. Is it a document, a book, a pamphlet, a museum piece, a photoduplicate, or what? Whatever is done to it in the process of permanent addition to a collection depends to a great degree on the nature of the record.

Chances are that it may require some kind of cleaning, perhaps even fumigating. Silverfish, lice, and other destructive insects that may have imbedded themselves should be eradicated and obliterated. Special care, however, should be exercised that in cleansing and fumigation no harm will come to the material itself.

After the substance has been declared "clean" and thus ready to be brought into close proximity with other archival-historical resources, the sometimes painstaking sorting, identification, and ordering of the entire collection must follow. The order in which papers have been received will be retained if at all possible. At this stage, however, it is well to assume that not all of the items will be added permanently to the collection.

A clear title to the materials and resources must accompany their receipt. Answers to the following questions must be readily available in writing:

- [ ] Who is the present owner of the collection? Does he have the total right to transfer this ownership to a church depository?
- [ ] Does he have the legal right to transfer also all copyrights inherent in the resources?
- [ ] What, in his opinion, is the historical significance of the collection? Why?
- [ ] Who were previous owners?
- [ ] What physical description of the materials, including quantity, is available?
- [ ] What is the purpose for the transaction — loan, study, examination, identification, view to purchase, exhibition, exchange?
- [ ] What is the general condition of the materials — good, fair, poor?
- [ ] Are there any restrictions attached to the materials — eternal obligations to preserve, limited access granted, reference access only, no copying rights, no publicational rights?
- [ ] What are the obligations and responsibilities of the receiving institution, in view of any prospective future destruction, exchange, or transfer?

A receiving form such as the one shown in Figure I can easily be adapted to any agency. Its sensitive paper allows for any number of distribution copies: one for the original file, a "processing copy" to follow the collection through every step of processing including the final preparation of the index or catalogue, a "cross reference file" copy, a "collection copy" to remain with the collection, and an "audit copy" to be used at the end of the year for statistical purposes. Other copies could be made as needed.

The form further allows for an individual number, a brief description of the materials transmitted, identification of the historical significance, transfer of clear title, space for various optional services, a declaration of the contributor as to the kind of access permitted, accessioning date, notations about appraisal, inventory, and cataloging. Such forms, modified to the specific use of an agency and noting its peculiar interests, serve excellent purposes.

No material whatsoever should ever be received on a mere oral basis. The correspondence or a receiving record ought to testify clearly the conditions under which materials are transferred as outlined above. Nothing less than this, regardless of the vast amount of bookkeeping that it may require, will ever serve the purpose of preservation and use.

A qualification such as the following ought to be added to a receiving document: "The archives reserves the right to cull all collections transferred to it on the basis of this receiving record before adding them to the permanent collection or even after they have been added to the collections. Publicational rights are herewith also transferred to the archives without reservation." Agreements of receipt and transfer should specify whose right it is to decide destruction and retention. Many heartaches can be avoided if this is clarified.

Appendixes 1 and 2 are documents dealing with the deposit of congregational and other records at the Concordia Historical Institute. It is highly desirable for agencies transferring records to formulate an official resolution of the type suggested. Congregations should also file an application to transfer records, indicate precisely which records are included and the reason for transfer, cite the text of the resolution, and outline access to the materials; officials of the congregation should authorize the transfer. In general, it is better for a religious archives to discourage indefinite loans than to solicit them unless the archivist anticipates permanent ownership of

Concordia Historical Institute
DEPARTMENT OF ARCHIVES AND HISTORY
THE LUTHERAN CHURCH - MISSOURI SYNOD
801 DE MUN AVENUE ESTABLISHED 1847 • INCORPORATED 1927 ST. LOUIS, MISSOURI 63105

RECEIVING RECORD

1442

FROM:	DATE:
ADDRESS:	

MATERIALS TRANSMITTED (BOOKS, RECORDS, PERSONAL PROPERTY):	NUMBER OF CARTONS:

HISTORICAL SIGNIFICANCE:

Purpose for transmitting materials:

1. [ ] Contribution, unconditional

The Concordia Historical Institute reserves the right to cull all individual items and collections transferred to it through this receiving form before or after adding them to the permanent files. Copy and literary rights are herewith also transferred without reservation to the Institute. Items transferred are an irrevocable gift.

Signature of donor or courier: _____

2. [ ] Book Sales (obtain signature, Bulletin #7) and attach

0. [ ] Exchange (On back, nature of)

4. [ ] Loan (obtain signature, Bulletin #15) and attach

Purpose of loan: □ Examination □ Study □ Identification □ View to Purchase
 □ Exhibition □ Other (Specify)_____

_____

PREVIOUS OWNERS?

CONDITION: GENERALLY □ GOOD □ FAIR □ POOR

DONOR GRANTS: □ UNRESTRICTED USE	□ LIMITED ACCESS	SEALED UNTIL (DATE) □
CORRESPONDENCE ON THIS □ YES □ NO	NAME	DATE OF CSS
HOW SHIPPED?	POSTAGE, INSURANCE & OTHER COSTS?	
RECEIVED BY STAFF:	APPRAISAL ATTACHED (NAME AND DATE)	
PRELIMINARY INVENTORY PREPARED (NAME AND DATE)	COLLECTION ACCESSIONED (NAME AND DATE)	INDEX OR CATALOGUE PREPARED (NAME AND DATE)

PRINTED BY THE STANDARD REGISTER COMPANY, U.S.A.

Figure 1: Receiving forms expedite accessioning.

valuable and irreplacable resources. Short-term loans for research study or exhibit should be carefully documented.

Accessioning and Registration

Two primary objectives govern registration or accessioning of historical resources and materials. The first takes into account the need for identification of the source or origin of the materials. If the reasons for the transmission have been outlined as indicated above, the accessioning process at this time merely will identify a specific letter or book as having come from the source or office indicated on the receiving record. This can become extremely crucial when, for example, in a pamphlet there are all kinds of marginalia. A researcher will soon ask, "Whose comments are these? Who was the former owner who disagreed with a statement and said so?" If a page is missing, if there are legal complications, or if there are certain restrictions imposed on the use of the materials by the donors, the individual document will not state all of this information, but the accessioning record will identify such restrictions. If textual criticism becomes necessary the archivist can return to the original contributor for additional information. In summary, therefore, the first purpose of the accessioning or registration process is to permanently identify a given item as to the manner, circumstances, and source of receipt.

The second objective is to record all materials that have been received as accurately, quickly, and permanently as possible. If this is not done, there may be legal complications and responsibilities that cannot be discharged. For example, a family, a board, or an institution may suddenly need to know whether its materials had been received. A good accessioning procedure will reveal this immediately. A donor file listing the names and addresses of all those who have made material contributions to the collections is helpful.

But how does a religious archives achieve both of these objectives with the minimum time and effort? Especially if the registrar or person responsible for accessioning is not employed on a full-time basis, every possible corner needs to be cut that does not materially contribute to the work. Here again, there are several basic considerations.

☐ The entire accessioning process must be accomplished as quickly and as effortlessly as possible.

☐ Any system that causes hindrances and delays ultimately becomes detrimental and un-

workable. Such delays are often cumulative; the rainy day to catch up seldom comes.

☐ Unaccessioned material ought never to be allowed into the hands of the researchers, officials, or anyone else. This makes it imperative that the accessioning process be expedited.

☐ An accessioning procedure that immediately identifies the contributor of the materials and the collection itself is absolutely essential. Unaccessioned materials that are not properly identified are confusing, and recovering background information and data may be impossible later.

Having looked at these basic principles, consider now procedures for the permanent identification of the object or papers received. First of all, identifying marks should be placed, wherever possible, directly on the object itself. Labels or tags cannot serve as a substitute. In fact, any other identification marks, regardless of how they are applied, if impermanent or in danger of being separated from the object, should never be used.

Ideally, therefore, the archivist should work with a coding system that will occupy only a tiny amount of space. Many objects may not have sufficient space on which to write details. A unique number or code, like the fingerprints of an individual, can be imposed on each item received. Otherwise confused and garbled information may result, making any checkback or route study impossible.

The substances used in registering items may vary with the materials registered. Dorothy H. Dudley and Irma Bezold in *Museum Registration Methods* (Washington, D.C.:American Association of Museums, 1958) list India ink, waterproofing ink, artists oil colors, and various other substances for marking materials. Naturally, glass objects are far more difficult to inscribe than paper.

In the case of papers of all kinds, manuscripts, documents, books, and pamphlets, never, under any circumstances, should the text of the document be marred or obliterated. The information to be added on such a document should be kept at a bare minimum and as small as possible, especially if the usable white space is limited. The identification should list the donor or source of purchase, the new owner of the material, and the date received. Each individual piece should thus be identified.

The question remains whether in a larger collection such as the files of a regional home mission board or similar agencies, each resource, letter, or document should be assigned a specific number immediately at the time of accessioning, or whether this can be added subsequently. It is hard to generalize. The above requirements of accessioning should be met regardless of the time sequence, but processing collections quickly is usually most important.

If every margin and other white space on a document has been used up and codification would obliterate part of the text, it is best to place the document into an acid-free folder or sleeve and apply the identification to it.

In the actual codification a combination of letters and numerals represents two or three initials of a donor, abbreviations for the month and year, and a sequential numbering series. The code for each item should immediately reveal the following information:

☐ The name of the archives or institution receiving the materials — branding the item as belonging to the new agency — and the address in case the materials are lost or stolen. Abbreviations may be used if intelligible.

☐ The donor's name, such as an individual, institution, or agency. The initial letters of the words in the name can be used.

☐ The date of receipt.

☐ The accession number, added for further identification and appearing as a unique, individual number of that one particular item exclusively. If the accessioning ledger is set up so that a numerical series is begun with each month, the processing will be expedited. The accessioner will not have to wait until the previous two or three months' accessioning has been completed before continuing a numerical series in sequence. If a numerical series of accessions follows throughout an entire year, it will be impossible to continue any accessioning process until every previous item has been accessioned. By beginning a new numbering series with each month the registrar can temporarily pass over a heavy volume of receipts.

All of these matters are safeguards for preserving the integrity of the collection and the individual item. Should a document ever become orphaned from its collection, it can quickly be replaced without much loss of time. The researcher may also wish to make use of this data for fast and easy identification.

Stamping devices are readily available and save a lot of routine writing. Date stamps on a band, prepared in various sizes, can be purchased from any stationery supply store. The same is also true of a large banded stamp, containing all of the letters of the alphabet in three or four rows. This can be used to reproduce the initials of the donor, board, or agency. The name stamp, together with the date stamp, should be used both in the accessioning ledger and on the papers transmitted.

The stamping devices, especially if self-inking, form an excellent combination with the stamp identifying the archival agency and its address. A numbering device, stamping the same number twice, once in the accessioning ledger and again on the document, will complete the tools the accessioner needs and will expedite the process of document identification that is so necessary in a day when thievery has increased.

Next consider ledger registration, accessions sheets, and the donor index. Such forms, regardless of how they are being maintained, should ultimately be available only in permanently bound form. Either begin with a bound ledger, or if sheets are used bind them permanently at certain intervals. These forms should contain the identical codes and whatever information is necessary for a permanent record. The conditions of transmission, potential use, and any restrictions should be listed. It should yield a complete description of the materials accessioned. Don't write a book each time a new item is added, nor copy out the entire contents of a document. However, provide enough detail for precise identification fifty years after the entry. A check might become necessary much sooner than it may appear today. If the donor has given a complete description, it may be easier to inscribe this into the ledger than to work up a new one. However, actually compare the donor's description with the document to ascertain whether they fully agree. The donor's description may be based upon hearsay or family tradition and thus may not be completely accurate. The receiving record will make it much easier for the accessioner to give the detailed description necessary. If materials have been transferred by mail with an accompanying letter, this should also be used in accessioning.

If the accessioning receipts are being maintained on the basis of a numerical sequence starting with one at the beginning of each month, the exact total will be available at the end of each month; at the end of the year, the grand total can be obtained by adding the twelve monthly totals.

It will be helpful and save time to prepare a card on each accession for the donor file. The date of the receipt of materials, accession number, and, if desirable, a brief description of each item will prove to be extremely valuable as this information takes on cumulative form. If you haven't already experienced the granddaughter's request to see "grandpa's watch" given to your agency twenty-five years ago, you may not be as badly in need of a donor file.

The receiving records or transmission documents should be filed alphabetically, as correspondence involved in the transaction. Again, be sure you get the signature of the individual who turns over valued property to you. Such a signature is essential, and no material whatever should be received on a purely oral basis.

Filing Principles

All kinds of filing systems are workable and usable. The important thing is to select and establish a system and stick with it. Alterations, modifications, and changes in a system, once in use, become costly and cause confusion. Most systems in existence are based on some rational order, sometimes numerical, sometimes alphabetical, and frequently a combination of both. Even though there may be hundreds of schemes that are adaptable, the filing system employed by an archives agency will be unique and appropriate to it alone.

The first task in developing a filing system is to prepare an administrative chart of the offices or departments that are served by the archives agency. This chart should note interrelations that exist between them and other administrative offices, agencies, and entities. Prepare the chart in such a fashion that all records-creating offices are fully identified. Place all entities on the chart so that the administrative structure will become apparent. This will become the key to your files.

Once you have established the current administrative structure, you have, actually, prepared your filing scheme or the sequence in which your records should be stored. After completing the contemporary description, backtrack and identify all antecedent structures and list them by creation date and purpose as well. This process will introduce you to the second major tool, which is the preparation of a brief history of each one of the offices, departments, agencies, and boards. Identify their creation dates, objectives, and development. Indicate also the creating authority, responsibilities, and any modifications of this structure made over the years. List as many names and dates as possible. From the history and the adminstrative chart, most of the important names, dates, and changes in function, title, and objectives will be apparent. Any additional commentary that may be needed can be researched later.

The user with knowledge of the history of an agency, organization, or institution served by the archives can sometimes identify major sources of information independently, even without consulting a key, if the subjects are well specified. This saves the researcher and the staff much time.

The basic principles of arrangement to be applied to the files and resources in your custody are often referred to as "provenance" and "respect des fonds." Records must be grouped according to the individual, office, or administrative unit that created or accumulated them, and the arrangement imposed by the creators themselves should be preserved by the archival institution. Hence, do not destroy or radically change the filing order employed by the creating office. Retain the files in the order in which they were created and used. Such arrangements are easily maintained because they normally do not require any intricacies of cross reference or cataloging.

It is best to work with the records group system described in many books and articles elsewhere. It divides the records of an archives into major components identifying each one of them as a record group. Each one of these records groups can then be subdivided into as many series as necessary, and the series subdivided into individual folders and the folders into discrete items. Detailed assistance in this archival function can be found in David B. Gracy's *Archives and Manuscripts: Arrangement and Description*, a volume of the Basic Manual Series published by the Society of American Archivists.

Description

Every religious archives should develop types of finding aids suitable for its collections and the uses for which the records are preserved. The purpose of a system of finding aids is to provide essential information about the holdings of the archives for its patrons and researchers and to enable the staff to retrieve records. It is more important to describe all collections, even if briefly, than to describe only some resources in great detail. Common types of finding aids include guides, inventories and registers, card catalogs, special lists, accessions registers, indexes, and calendars. The personal services of a knowledgeable archivist and a helpful reference staff will always be essential to the researcher. Good descriptive tools, nevertheless, make your holdings more accessible.

7
Reference Service

Tension constantly faces the archivist in the twin obligations to preserve and serve. The archivist who is overly protective of the collections will discourage service; the one who serves with reckless abandon may destroy. A collection that may not be consulted and searched has no value whatsoever — unless it is in a space capsule, not to be opened until a millenium hence. Equally tragic, however, is the historical collection that is profligately squandered through destructive research. What the archivist needs imperatively is a delicate balance so that the agency may preserve and retain for posterity but at the same time vigorously provide services satisfying both casual query and in-depth research.

Assisting Researchers

Several prohibitions and precautions help to achieve a balance in reference services. First, researchers ought to be carefully screened so that the archivist is convinced that each is capable of serious, competent research. Forms, devised for that purpose, can be extremely useful; an example appears as Appendix 3.

Second, make sure the researcher understands the established house rules consisting of the method and manner in which materials and resources may be used, copied, or photographically reproduced. Obtain testimony of the researcher's responsibility and accountability in a signed statement.

Third, make the collections available for use only in specifically designated supervised areas, preferably apart from the stacks. No researcher, under any condition, should ever be permitted to scrounge around or rifle in the collections at random.

Fourth, discuss publication privileges in advance. It is always wise to exercise every precaution when copies — by hand, typewriter, or camera — are made of sources. The physical security of the item must be protected and the rights of the original owner and the archival agency preserved. Request that proper credit be given the archives as well as the

donor when use has been made of collections. Anything less could be considered ungrateful or dishonest. Emphasize that photoduplicates are made only as a service to the individual researcher, not as a publication that might violate copyrights.

Restrictions on Access

Religious archives, like secular institutions, reserve the right to impose certain restrictions on access to specific collections. Generally, three categories of availability are recognized. Open materials are available to any qualified researcher; restricted materials can be used only under particular conditions; and sealed or closed materials are not available for research for a predetermined period of time.

Collections are closed or restricted for various reasons, but the most important ones for a religious archives are to protect the physical integrity of the materials and to protect the privacy of living persons named in the records. The particular conditions of access applied to restricted collections vary. Perhaps the material may be used freely but not photocopied. Perhaps direct quotations from some sources are prohibited. Perhaps researchers may use the files for statistical studies as long as individuals are not identified. Some archival agencies reserve the right to read any manuscript produced before it is published to ensure that the rules of access have been followed.

Even in the case of closed collections, exceptions must be made in accordance with the "right to know" principle. For example, the designated official representative of a component of the religious body served by the archives who has demonstrated a legitimate purpose, namely an inquiry into matters as to the accountability of the ecclesiastical agent, who is pursuing this purpose in a reasonable way, has a "right to know." Exceptions might also be made in another case, if the need to know is great and a specific request for access serves the best interest of the people involved.

The administration of restrictions on access requires experience and good judgment from the archivist. Historical research is best served by open archival collections. Sealed materials should be closed for as short a period of time as possible, and other restrictions should be imposed only when necessary. Any restrictions should be worked out with the donor or records-creating office before materials are transferred. They must be clearly stated in the accession record and in other finding aids. A researcher who visits a well-managed religious archives dedicated to preservation and to service will realize that access to the records is a privilege.

A modern research room contains microfilm readers, finding aids, reference material, and working space for researchers. Photos courtesy of the Department of Archives and History, Concordia Historical Institute.

Priorities in Reference Service

Ever since *Roots* and other accounts of family history, the number of genealogists and family historians has multiplied by leaps and bounds. You, too, will be bombarded with telephone calls and mail queries. Be prepared to offer guidance and assistance. Emphasize that as much information as possible must first be gathered from immediate family members, and that thereafter correspondence may be helpful as well as research in various depositories. A file in the religious archives of biographies, autobiographies, and obituaries will be valuable to the genealogist. Records searchers and certified genealogists may also be helpful, at least in rendering counsel and aid. The least the archivist ought to do is to refer the inquiry to an agency or individual who may be able to help.

A religious archivist could, in rendering service, view the clientele in this order of priority.
□ Officers and administrative units of the church
□ Church-related seminaries, colleges, and other institutions
□ Local congregations
□ Scholars and academicians
□ Family historians and genealogists

Another archivist might serve congregational needs first. The priorities may well vary, depending on the nature of the collections and the charter of the archives.

Fees

Under certain circumstances it may be necessary to require fees for the performance of certain tasks. Photoduplication or copywork should be the financial responsibility of the client. Charges for services performed for others in reference and research, after some gratis time is used for consultation and demonstration, may be legitimate. Theological and family historical research is usually performed at a predetermined rate. The important aspect of charges is to notify the client in advance and outline the circumstances under which they are imposed. It is always well before imposing any service charge to study the matter very thoroughly, making certain that there is no discrimination involved, and that the cash income will, indeed, offset the staff time that has been spent and the out-of-pocket expenses that have been incurred. Special considerations should also be made for reciprocal services.

Helping the Parish

The religious archivist can be of great service to local parishes or congregations under all kinds of circumstances. You will most likely receive a hurried, frantic telephone call or letter from the person appointed to write the church history for an anniversary celebration. All of your expertise in research and knowledge of the history of the communion will be drawn upon. The caller will indicate that all their original records were "burned" or "lost." In many cases you will have ample resources available about that parish and consequently will have to determine how much time you may be able to spend in the search. Acknowledge such inquiries immediately, and insert a questionnaire asking the caller for the basic information essential to the history of the parish. The congregation fills this questionnaire in and returns it to the archives to save the archivist from duplicating information already available to them. On any number of occasions an archivist has conducted painstaking research and submitted a report to the parish, only to learn they already knew that, and were really seeking answers to some new questions. The questionnaire can be a safeguard for avoiding dismaying duplication.

The archivist may also wish to offer suggestions to the local parish about additional sources or records that could be used to complete the history. Such sources would include local newspapers, the records in the county courthouse, and monographs. The archivist should also stand ready to offer additional suggestions for celebrating anniversaries. Some ideas might include a display of museum pieces, a project to gather cemetery records, a photography contest, a pageant, drama, or music festival.

More fundamental, however, for the archival-historical well-being of a parish is your recommendation that the congregation or local group establish the office of archivist. Then assist that person with guidelines of various types, lists of items to be preserved, methods of preservation, and also suggestions for a salvage operation in event of a catastrophe. It is also well to have on hand guidelines for the restoration and rehabilitation of local historical sites and buildings. In return, often people within the parish can also be enlisted as volunteers for translating foreign language documents, conducting oral history programs, developing photographic files, and searching for special documents, serials, and artifacts for your archives.

Loans

Under no circumstances should an archivist ever lend any item, whether document, pamphlet, book, or photograph, unless a duplicate is immediately at hand or obtainable. Loans without safeguards face hazards making it unlikely that they will be returned in good condition.

It is far better to serve the patrons through photoduplication or loan of microfilm. In such cases, a service charge to pay for the handling and shipping costs may be appropriate. Through the production of bibliographies or by sharing bibliographic references, the patron ought to be encouraged to use local libraries and depositories, and perhaps to try interlibrary loans wherever possible.

8
Photoduplicating and Microfilming

Volumes have been written about microfilming and photoduplication work, and the reader is advised to consult them. This section will briefly outline some of the cares and cautions.

Not everything is worth reproducing photographically. Duplicates may be available quite readily. In other cases, materials themselves may be intrinsically less important historically. Perhaps the potential use of the item does not warrant its reproduction. The primary reasons for microfilming or photoduplication are security, availability, preservation of originals, and greater access.

Before plunging into a program of photographically reproducing materials, check the copyright laws. Because works are equally covered whether or not they are published, copyright applies to manuscripts as well as printed articles or books. The duration of the copyright protection applies from the creation of the work, whether or not it is published.

For works created on or after 1 January 1978, copyright endures for the life of the author plus fifty years. After the death of the author, the heirs or anyone to whom the rights were willed owns the copyright. If a work is prepared by two or more authors, the copyright endures for the life of the last surviving author plus fifty years.

If a work is made for hire as part of an employee's job, the copyright is held by a corporation or organization rather than an individual, and the copyright lasts seventy-five years from its first publication or one hundred from its creation, whichever expires first.

Unpublished manuscripts created before 1 January 1978, when the new law went into effect, come under the same provisions as stated above, except that all such works are protected at least until 31 December 2002.

Copyright protection gives the owner of the copyright the authority to control or restrict all copying or publication of the work. The law has provided certain exceptions for libraries and archives for fair use by scholars. There are many detailed provisions, but basically they mean that single copies may be made without the permission of the copyright owner for purposes of study and for library and archives to obtain copies of such works for their collections. In most instances today, the production of microfilm is considered a publication having also the implications of copyright.

Note that resources should be microfilmed or xeroxed only when they are essential for the use of the patron or required for security purposes. Without such guidelines, most religious archives would not be able to fund any photoduplication programs at all.

Always be prepared to apply the proper credit and bibliographical essentials to the copies, and carefully abide by agreements made with other depositories whose permission may be necessary for copying. Indiscriminate photoduplication should be avoided, and archival agencies should at all times endeavor to provide the necessary safeguards and controls over the materials at their disposal.

Guidelines for Filming

Unless a religious archives has its own professional microfilming staff, equipment, and laboratory, it should secure the services of a good commerical firm. In either case, the following standards ought to be observed scrupulously.

A. General Requirements
   1. *Film type.* All film must be permanent record, fine grain, high contrast, panchromatic 35mm., unperforated safety film, manufactured especially for documentary or archival reproductions. The negative films should meet the requirements of the American National Standards Institute for permanent microphotographic copy.

2.   *Illumination.* Equipment used must be such as to ensure even illumination over the entire area of the document being photographed. Periodic checks should be made with a light meter to ensure consistent illumination.

3.   *Background Density.* The background transmission density on a negative film must be between 1.0 and 1.3 especially where negatives are to be used for positive microfilm or xerox reproduction.

4.   *Density Variation.* The variation of background density in any one image must not exceed plus or minus 2.5% of the average density except where variation is caused by stains or discolorations. Variation of background density within any one row shall not exceed plus or minus 15% of the most common background density.

5.   *Resolution.* The resolution of processed negative film must show at least 100 (preferably higher) lines per mm. in the center of the image. Positive copies made from negatives must have a resolution of at least 90% of the minimum negative resolution. The third generation should have at least 80% of the minimum.

6.   *Processing.* Films must be processed according to the American National Standards Institute for films of permanent records, and periodic tests must be made to ensure that the residual hypo content of the processed film does not exceed 0.005 mg. per square inch.

7.   *Reduction Ratio.* Unless otherwise indicated use as low a reduction ratio as possible since this makes for sharper work.

B.   Microfilming Procedure

1.   Each film must begin and end with three feet of unexposed film.

2.   All films must be wound on standard plastic spools of the Universal Taylor Reel type.

3.   Pages mutilated by the loss of a portion of the page must have the lost portion revealed by backing the page with a sheet of white paper.

4.   Wherever possible, especially in the case of manuscript material, each page of the material should be numbered consecutive-ly through the entire unit of material for later identification purposes.

5.   *Initial and Terminal Targets.* Each film must begin and end with the targets, and the arrangements must be as follows:

a.   Identification target. This brief title or resume of contents must be filmed so as to be visible to the naked eye without magnification.

b.   The target of the agency. This includes the sponsor's name and copyright restrictions.

c.   Bibliographical Information Target. This includes title, table of contents, location of the original material, name of filming company, etc.

d.   The target START. This must be filmed with a six-inch ruler and at the same reduction ratio as the material itself.

e.   The main body of material.

f.   The target END. This must appear at the end of the film or at the end of each unit of material on the roll.

6.   If more than one item or unit of material is to be filmed on one roll, the above targets must be filmed at the beginning and at the end of each item or unit of material. The bibliographical information target will determine what constitutes each item or unit of material. A different bibliographical information target will be included for each item or unit of material. About six inches of unexposed film must appear between each such item or unit of material.

7.   *Internal Targets.* The following targets are to be inserted into the material, when applicable, at their proper places:

a.   Frame Identification Target. In all material where there is no page identification or running page titles, a frame identification target must be inserted at the bottom of every frame.

b.   The target CONTINUED must be used at the end of the film if the material is to be continued on another roll. In such cases at the beginning of the next roll, the target START must be replaced by the target CONTINUED.

c. The target ILLEGIBLE must be used when the original is illegible. The illegible material must also be filmed for the sake of completeness.

d. The target BLANK must be inserted when blank pages are omitted in the filming. The number of pages omitted are to be indicated on the target.

e. The target MISSING is to be used when pages are missing or when larger gaps appear in the material. The missing pages number must be indicated on the target.

8. When a division or break occurs within a given bibliographic unit of material, it is to be indicated by a gap of several frames of unexposed film.

C. Processing of film

1. Immediately upon receipt, check the film carefully for its contents, legibility, and mechanical errors.

2. Provide the film with the sequential accession or file number.

3. Include the contents in your indexing process, at least as far as the film number, source of the film, brief description of the contents, date received and purchase price, filming company, availability of the positive and/or negative, location of the original materials, and the number of feet on the film. Further indexing can take place later.

The same principles would certainly also apply to any other photoduplication process. The archivist, like a good historian, must specifically document any copies made in order to assure their authenticity.

9
Exhibits

Displays and exhibits in archives? Yes, even archives have a need for good exhibits! Such displays become the bait in the mousetrap that will create a deeper interest and concern in historical matters. Without exhibits, an archives can soon convey the image of an old "musty, dusty closet." People are fascinated by special documents, drawings, embellishments on documents, illuminations, and archival and manuscript resources. The exhibit can be considerably enhanced if unique museum pieces and artifacts or unusual books can be displayed together with the documents. Hence a museum collection complementing the archives is of great importance.

Ordinarily, do not display original materials or items of great intrinsic value. They can easily fade and deteriorate in direct sun or fluorescent light. Worse, they could be stolen or destroyed.

When planning an exhibit, develop it within the scope of your resources, documenting the services that you render, showing the type of material you hope to obtain. Displays should serve as good public relations. What kind of an exhibit would best tell the story of your purposes, objectives, and services? How could you demonstrate to the visitors the gaps you have in your collections and your need for their help to fill them? How can you widen the horizons of the visitors by interesting them in the history of your religious group? How can you lead them to read about some individual or event in ecclesiastical history?

After you have determined that, it will be well for you to consider security precautions that ought to be taken, management of traffic flow, atmospheric conditions, and the protection of the items displayed.

In designing displays, try to anticipate who your visitors will be. Which age group would be most likely to come? What are their personal interests, their physical abilities, their financial status? Which staff member could best identify with the majority of your visitors, make them feel welcome, and enable them to enjoy their experience?

These suggestions may be helpful.

☐ Never exhibit anything that has not been completely accessioned and brought under inventory controls. Keep a complete record of everything on display.

☐ Provide for detailed reference files on the material considered for display and also a

Widen the horizons of your visitors by interesting them in the history of your religious group. Right: Nursing sisters at work during the Spanish-American War. Photo courtesy of the Archives, Sisters of Mercy of the Union. Below: The congregation of a small rural church shortly after the 1890s. Photo courtesy of the Historical Commission of the Southern Baptist Convention. Next page: Girls dancing and boys' cooking class, Jewish Manual Training School, Chicago. Photos courtesy of Chicago Jewish Archives, Asher Library, Spertus College of Judaica.

photographic record of the museum items so that they may be thoroughly identified while they are separated from the collection or their storage area.

☐ Prepare your exhibits with a unified theme. The exhibit theme may be compared to the subject covered in a book. Such an exhibit, like a book, requires an introduction and may have several parts or chapters. A display case or room, for example, could constitute the unified whole.

☐ An exhibit should never look like an antique shop where a half dozen oil lamps, pairs of gay '90s boots, and dozens of candlesticks are displayed on a shelf. Rather, assemble the artifacts as meaningfully as possible in a setting where they replicate their original use.

☐ Endeavor to make the exhibit as arresting, thought-provoking, and educational as possible. This can be accomplished with the use of color, design of movement by arrangement, asymmetrical forms, contrast, and other principles of good design.

☐ Descriptive captions should be attractively done and as brief as possible. The average museum visitor, it has been found, spends considerably less than a minute reading a single caption, and in slow reading at that! The item displayed together with the caption ought to trigger imagination and arouse curiosity so that the visitor may be induced to see and read more.

☐ Distribute literature or a memento at a special display.

☐ Issue announcements and invitations to your exhibit.

The above suggestions show that much time must be spent in preparing and organizing a display. Begin planning your exhibit by listing the objectives you wish to achieve, and then conduct extensive historical research. Finally, after this has been completed, ascertain the museum items that will illustrate the story you are planning to tell. It will be helpful to construct miniatures of the entire display or to rough out the artwork, captions, and the illustrative materials to envision how all will fit together. As much as space allows, visitors should be prohibited from viewing the housekeeping chores normally involved in the process of assembling a good exhibit.

Give consideration to offering museum extension services. Why not develop several kits of typical materials dealing with the pioneer period of the church, or worship materials, or foreign mission resources? Such kits could also contain ideas for a display in a local parish, making use of unique resources such as flags, posters, historically or ethnically popular clothing, and books of worship in various languages. A multimedia slide and sound presentation could also be most helpful. Ideas such as these are not only useful for educational purposes, but they also promote good public relations. A good book for the beginner is Armenta Neal's *Exhibits for the Small Museum*, published by the American Association for State and Local History.

10
Publications

A religious archives can extend its ability to serve, acquire new resources, promote its activities, and develop an excellent educational program with its publications. Consider printing and disseminating house organs, newsletters, scholarly journals, and publicity and promotional materials; consider using your denominational press.

Archivists of religious collections no less than others need to acquaint their constituencies with the collections and services they provide. Failure to do this restricts almost every area of their activity and leads to low budgets, a low status, low salaries, and a diminution of interest in the history of a religious institution. On the other hand, a vigorous information program can go a long way in overcoming handicaps and the limitations that may seem to serve as the parameters of an agency.

The religious archivist should consider several types of publications.

☐ Reports are essential. The archivist ought to report regularly on acquisitions, unique and unusual manuscript holdings, reference activities, research and counseling services, correspondence, preservation activities, staff matters, exhibits, and the variety of other activities and events that take place from week to week.

☐ Newsletters may be extremely helpful in keeping your "company of friends" informed periodically of the latest developments. Share special news of meetings, workshops, and research results in its pages. Keep it short and interesting.

☐ You may not be able to publish a scholarly journal because of the expenses involved and staff required. Nevertheless, several denominational historical journals have appeared for many years. The five oldest are: the *American Jewish Historical Quarterly,* published since 1893; the *Journal of Presbyterian History,* since 1901; the *Catholic Historical Review,* since 1915; the (Lutheran) *Concordia Historical Institute Quarterly,* since 1928; and the *Magazine of the Protestant Episcopal Church,* since 1932. A journal can serve your purposes excellently by disseminating the very substances of your collections. It may not be wise to direct it exclusively to the academic world, but rather to the average denominational reader and supporter of your agency. With good journalism, good make-up and design, and good illustrations and color, such a periodical can be self-sustaining. Even if a subsidy is required, it may still be worth the effort.

☐ A bulletin service can deal with various topics, informational and technical, which may be of interest to your clientele. Bulletins need not be issued periodically, and the format may vary.

☐ Posters are readily usable on church bulletin boards, in schools, in public meeting places, and the like. They call attention to archives exhibits, new acquisitions, or special services.

☐ Special brochures and leaflets are often very effective for your messages.

☐ Develop news stories and press releases, but again, as in exhibit design, be aware of the public you hope to serve. To get stories printed and disseminated, establish and cultivate good working relationships with the editors and be aware of the objectives of their newspapers or magazines.

Every occasion ought to be utilized to tell your story in any circumstances possible. Only then will the word get out who you are, what you have, and what you are trying to achieve. *The American Archivist* has published articles from time to time dealing with public relations of an archives agency, and the reader is encouraged to consult them. The best public relations, of course, is the prompt and expeditious answering of all mail and courteous and cheerful assistance. Rendering good service should be the mission of every religious archives.

Bibliography

Brichford, Maynard. *Archives and Manuscripts: Appraisal and Accessioning.* Chicago: Society of American Archivists, 1977.

Deutrich, Mabel E. "American Church Archives: An Overview." *American Archivist* 24:387-402 (0 61).

Fleckner, John. *Archives and Manuscripts: Surveys.* Chicago: Society of American Archivists, 1977.

Gingerich, Melvin. "An Effective Acquisitions Program for the Religious Archives." *American Archivist* 29:515-522 (0 66).

Gracy, David B. *Archives and Manuscripts: Arrangement and Description.* Chicago: Society of American Archivists, 1977.

Holbert, Sue E. *Archives and Manuscripts: Reference and Access.* Chicago: Society of American Archivists, 1977.

Schellenberg, T.R. *The Management of Archives.* New York: Columbia University Press, 1965.

Society of American Archivists. *Inventories and Registers: A Handbook of Techniques and Examples.* Chicago: Society of American Archivists, 1976.

Spence, Thomas H., Jr., Peterson, Virgil V., and O'Connor, Thomas F. "Church Archives and History." *American Association for State and Local History Bulletin* 1:257-304 (Ap 46).

Suelflow, August R. "Church Archives: Strengths and Weaknesses." Paper presented at the annual meeting of the Society of American Archivists, 1965.

—————. "Maximum and Minimum Standards for Religious Archives." *American Archivist* 32:225-229 (Jl 69).

—————. "Preserving Church Historical Resources." *American Archivist* 28:239-246 (Ap 65).

_____. "Records Management and Church Archives." *Records Management Journal* 5:30-34 (Wint 67).

_____. "The Churches Concern for Their History." *Moravian Theological Seminary Bulletin* (Fall 65), 1-12.

_____. "The Struggle of Church Archives for Respectability." *American Archivist* 24:403-408 (0 61).

Sweet, William B. "Church Archives in the United States." *American Archivist* 14:323-331 (0 51).

Varieur, Pascal M. "The Small, Limited, or Specialized Church Archives." *American Archivist* 24: 451-456 (0 61).

Walch, Timothy. *Archives and Manuscripts: Security*. Chicago: Society of American Archivists, 1977.

Warner, Robert M. "The Role of the Secular Institution in Collecting Church Records." *American Archivist* 28:247-254 (Ap 65).

Serials

The American Archivist. Published by the Society of American Archivists, 1937-Present.

Archives and History. Minutes and Reports of the Archivists' and Historians' Conference, Concordia Historical Institute, 1945-Present.

History News including *Technical Bulletins*. Published by the American Association for State and Local History, 1945-Present.

The Midwestern Archivist. Published by the Midwest Archives Conference, 1976-Present.

Prologue: The Journal of the National Archives. Published by the National Archives and Records Service, 1969-Present.

Appendix 1: Depositing Congregational Records

How are your congregation's records currently preserved? Are the necessary safeguards provided so that future generations will be able to use them as you are? Would you like some suggestions on what to preserve? We have a Bulletin (No. 2) which may be of help. Perhaps your congregation has given thought to microfilming or depositing your records in our synodical depository. We may be of service to your congregation if you have. Naturally, our deepest concern is for the proper care, preservation and use of such irreplaceable and invaluable historical resources.

Our primary purpose certainly is not to accumulate the manuscript records of the more than 5,000 congregations of The Lutheran Church — Missouri Synod. Under certain conditions, the Institute may, however, receive original manuscript records of congregations or synodically related organizations. Such records may include the minutes, ledgers of official acts, correspondence, charters, documents, constitutions, etc. Records, however, of a contemporary nature with current, operational value, *must* remain with the congregation for ready access. Historical records, on the other hand, may be received and filed in the archives under certain conditions. Basically, there are two plans by which this can be arranged:

1. As a permanent transfer of ownership to the Institute.
2. As a loan for an indeterminate term whereby the congregation retains ownership, but transfers custody of such records to the Institute.

The following policies shall be observed to avoid legal complications.

Permanent Transfer

If the Congregation desires to make a permanent transfer of its records to the Institute, it is essential that it provide for the following:

☐ The Congregation shall make application to the Institute to determine whether such records may be received, giving reasons for considering such transfer.
☐ The Application shall be signed by the pastor, the chairman and the secretary of the congregation.
☐ Such Application shall also contain the date and the text of the resolution adopted by the Congregation authorizing the transfer.

Suggested form of resolution:

RESOLVED: That the Voters' Assembly of _____, hereby assign all the right, title and interest of said Congregation in and to the Records described in the Application attached hereto to Concordia Historical

Reprinted from Aug. R. Suelflow, *Depositing Congregational Records*, Department of Archives and History Bulletin 12 (St. Louis: Concordia Historical Institute, 1965).

Institute, the official Department of Archives and History of The Lutheran Church — Missouri Synod, and that the proper officers of said Congregation, including the pastor, chairman, and secretary thereof, be authorized and directed, in the name and on behalf of the said Congregation, to execute any and all documents (including, but not limited to, the Application attached hereto, and the Congregational Records Transfer Agreement submitted by Concordia Historical Institute), and to do any and all things by them deemed necessary or proper to effectuate said transfer of ownership.

☐ Further, the Application shall contain a description of the content of each volume, ledger or paper indicating the number of pages and dates of each; shall state the historical importance of the records and their value; and shall give a description of their physical condition. (See Bulletin No. 12A.)

☐ The Director of the Institute may accept such Application and receive such Records when the above conditions have been met. The Institute and the Congregation shall then execute a Congregational Records Transfer Agreement in the form attached hereto.

Loan for an Indeterminate Term

Should a Congregation decide to transfer its records to the Institute on a loan basis, whereby the Congregation retains ownership, designating the Institute as the custodian for an indeterminate term, the following conditions shall be met:

☐ Application for a loan shall be made in writing, giving reasons for considering such transfer.

☐ The Application shall be signed by the pastor, the chairman and the secretary of the Congregation.

☐ Such Application shall contain the date and the text of the resolution adopted by the Congregation authorizing the loan of such records.

Suggested form of resolution:

RESOLVED: That the Voters' Assembly of _____ _____, hereby loan for an indeterminate term the Records of said Congregation described in the Application attached hereto to Concordia Historical Institute, the official Department of Archives and History of The Lutheran Church — Missouri Synod, and that the proper officers of said Congregation, including the pastor, chairman, and secretary thereof, be authorized and directed, in the name and on behalf of said Congregation, to execute any and all documents (including, but not limited to, the Application attached hereto, and the Congregational Records Loan Agreement submitted by Concordia Historical Institute), and to do any and all things by them deemed necessary or proper to effectuate said loan.

☐ Further, the Application shall state the restrictions as to use of such records, if any; shall contain a complete description of the contents of each volume, ledger, or paper, indicating the number of pages and the dates of each; shall state the historical importance of the records and their value; and shall give a description of their physical condition. (See Bulletin 12A.)

☐ The Congregation shall obligate itself to maintain the physical condition of the records, such as rebinding or rehabilitation, whenever this may become necessary in the opinion of the Director of the Institute.

☐ In view of the Congregation retaining ownership and using the Institute's staff and facilities, we urge that such a parish commit itself to an annual organization ($50.00 per year) membership.

☐ The Director of the Institute may accept such Application and receive such records from Congregations as a loan for an indeterminate term when the above conditions have been met. The Congregation and the Institute shall then execute a Congregational Records Loan Agreement in the form attached hereto.

We further solicit inquiries concerning these procedures and the deposit. Furthermore, we always welcome the opportunity to advise on the care and preservation of a Congregation's records in its own archives.

Bulletin 12 A

Application for:
TRANSFER
Of
CONGREGATIONAL RECORDS
to
Concordia Historical Institute
801 DeMun Avenue
St. Louis 5, Missouri

I. Name of Congregation: _____ Place: _____

_____

II. Nature of Transfer Sought: ( ) Permanent Transfer
                                       ( ) Permanent Loan

III. Description of Records:

Kind	No. of Vols. or Ledgers	No. of Pages	Dates from – to	Complete or Incomplete	Condition
A. Minutes	_____	_____	_____	_____	_____
B. Baptisms	_____	_____	_____	_____	_____
C. Funerals	_____	_____	_____	_____	_____
D. Marriages	_____	_____	_____	_____	_____
E. Confirmation	_____	_____	_____	_____	_____
F. Documents	_____	_____	_____	_____	_____

G. Content not listed in above categories: _____

_____

_____

IV. Reason for Seeking Transfer:

A. ( )   Inadequate Preservation Facilities
B. ( )   No longer of functional use to Congregation
C. ( )   Records have wide historical significance
D. ( )   Other: _____

_____

V. Official Resolution Authorizing Transfer:

A. Text of Resolution: _____

_____

_____

_____

_____

_____

_____

B. Resolution Recorded:
   Where: _____ Date: _____

page two
Bulletin 12 A

    VI. Use of Material
        We request that the materials be placed on:
            A.( )restricted use
            B.( )unrestricted use.

    VII. Signatures of Officials of Requesting Congregation:

            Pastor   _____

            Chairman   _____

            Secretary   _____

            Date   _____

(For Institute use only)

Request for transfer granted on basis of:

( ) Permanent Transfer ( ) Permanent Loan ( ) Other _____

            Signed _____, Director_____
                  Concordia Historical Institute

            Date _____

File No. and place assigned _____

Accession Nos. _____

CONGREGATIONAL RECORDS TRANSFER AGREEMENT

Bulletin #12B
July 1965

CONCORDIA HISTORICAL INSTITUTE
Department of Archives and History
The Lutheran Church--Missouri Synod
801 DeMun Avenue
St. Louis, Missouri 63105

This Agreement, entered into the _____ day of _____, 19____, by and between Concordia Historical Institute (herein called "Institute") and:

Name of Congregation: _____

Address: _____
(being herein referred to as "Congregation");

W I T N E S S E T H: That

WHEREAS, the Congregation has filed an Application with the Institute at 801 DeMun Avenue, St. Louis, Missouri 63105, for the permanent transfer of certain of the Congregation's Records to the Institute;

WHEREAS, the Institute has accepted the Congregation's said Application;

NOW, THEREFORE, it is covenanted and agreed by and between the parties hereto as follows:

1. Said Application and the Acceptance thereof, are attached hereto and made a part of this Agreement.

2. The Congregation hereby assigns all its right, title, and interest in and to the aforesaid Records to the Institute.

3. The Institute shall have full authority to retain, dispose of, or deal in said Records as the Institute's property without liability upon any ground whatsoever to the Congregation.

4. During such time as the Institute shall retain the unrestricted and unqualified ownership and custody of said Records, the Pastor of the Congregation, or any authorized member thereof, shall be permitted to inspect said Records at the aforesaid offices of the Institute upon reasonable notice to the Director of the Institute at such times as said Director may authorize.

_____
For the Congregation

_____
For the Institute

CONGREGATIONAL RECORDS LOAN AGREEMENT

Bulletin #12C
July 1965

CONCORDIA HISTORICAL INSTITUTE
Department of Archives and History
The Lutheran Church--Missouri Synod
801 DeMun Avenue
St. Louis, Missouri 63105

This Agreement, entered into the _____day of _____, 19_____,
by and between Concordia Historical Institute (herein called "Institute") and:

Name of Congregation: _____

Address: _____
(being herein referred to as "Congregation");

W I T N E S S E T H: That

WHEREAS, the Congregation has filed an Application with the Institute at
801 DeMun Avenue, St. Louis, Missouri 63105, for the loan of certain of the
Congregation's Records to the Institute for an indeterminate term;

WHEREAS, the Institute has accepted the Congregation's said Application;

NOW, THEREFORE, it is covenanted and agreed by and between the parties
hereto as follows:

1.   Said Application and the Acceptance thereof are attached hereto and
made a part of this Agreement.

2.   The possession of said Records loaned to the Institute by the
Congregation may be retained by the Institute until such time as the Congregation
terminates said loan as herein provided.

3.   The Congregation may terminate the loan of said Records at any time
by serving a written demand upon the Institute for the same (signed by the Pastor,
Chairman and Secretary of the Congregation), which written demand shall specify
a date of termination of said loan of not less than thirty (30) days after the service
of said written demand upon the Institute, and which written demand shall include
a certified copy of the resolution of the Voters' Assembly of the Congregation
authorizing such termination.

4.   The Congregation may obtain, upon the termination of the loan of said
Records in the aforesaid manner, or within sixty (60) days thereafter, the return of
said Records not theretofore returned to or abandoned by the Congregation as
provided herein, at the aforesaid offices of the Institute upon executing a receipt
for the same (signed by the Pastor, Chairman and Secretary of the Congregation.
If the Congregation desires to have said Records returned to the Congregation at an
address other than at the aforesaid offices of the Institute, the Congregation shall
designate such address in the aforesaid written demand for said Records. Upon
receiving such written instructions from the Congregation, the Institute shall return
said Records to the Congregation by depositing the same in the Unites States mails,

addressed to such address as the Congregation may designate, provided the Congregation has theretofore executed and delivered a receipt for said Records to the Institute, and deposited with the Institute such sum of money as the Institute shall deem necessary to cover the cost of packing, shipping and intransit insurance. If the Congregation fails to obtain the return of said Records within sixty (60) days after the termination of said loan, the term of said loan shall be deemed to be renewed by the parties hereto for an indeterminate term, and the Institute may retain said Records until such time as the Congregation terminates said loan and obtains the return of said Records in the manner provided above.

5. The Institute may, at its discretion, return any or all Records subject to this Agreement to the Congregation at any time, other than the time of termination of said loan by the Congregation (or renewal thereof), upon notifying the Pastor of the Congregation of such intent by registered letter, addressed to the address of the Congregation. If such registered letter is acknowledged by the Pastor of the Congregation, said Records shall be delivered to said Pastor at the aforesaid offices of the Institute upon the execution of a receipt for the same by said Pastor upon the date and at the time specified in said letter of notification. If such registered letter is not delivered to the Pastor of the Congregation, or, if delivered, is not acknowledged by said Pastor within thirty (30) days of the mailing of the same, or if delivered and acknowledged by said Pastor but said Pastor fails to execute a receipt for the same at the time and in the manner aforesaid, then in any of such events, said Records shall be deemed to have been abandoned by the Congregation, and all right, title and interest in and to such Records shall be deemed to have vested in the Institute with full authority to retain, dispose of, or deal in said Records as the Institute's property without liability upon any ground whatsoever to the Congregation.

6. The Congregation may transfer ownership of the Records to the Institute at any time upon the consent of the Institute.

7. The Institute shall not be required to insure the Records loaned to it by the Congregation for any purpose. The Institute shall not be liable for the deterioration or damage occurring to said Records through the normal aging process, usage, handling, acts of God and of nature; or for the safe keeping of such Records beyond the exercise of such precautions as are now in force, or may hereafter be put in force, for the safe keeping and preservation of the Records of the Institute itself.

8. The Congregation shall prepay or reimburse the Institute, at such times and in such amounts as the Director of the Institute may require, for the reasonable costs of properly maintaining and preserving said Records, including, but not by way of limitation, the costs of cleaning, repairing and restoring said Records.

9. The Institute is authorized to mark said Records with identification numbers, provided that reasonable care is exercised to apply marks that will not be injurious to said Records.

10. The Institute agrees to abide by such limitations as to the use of said Records as may be provided in the Application attached hereto, and made a part of this Agreement.

11.   The Institute reserves the right to file, index, and catalogue said Records in its regular filing, indexing and cataloguing system. If separate filing, indexing and cataloguing of said Records be maintained by the Institute, such files, indexes and catalogues may be nonetheless housed in conjunction with the general card catalogue.

12.   While said Records are in the possession and custody of the Institute they may be photographed, copied, or otherwise reproduced at the discretion of the Institute, whether or not for the profit of the Institute, provided, however, that authorization to photograph or otherwise copy said objects for the profit of any person other than the Institute shall not be given by the Institute without written permission from the Congregation.

13.   This Agreement and the covenants herein contained shall be binding upon the successors and assigns of the parties hereto. No modification, exception, or change in this Agreement may be made except by written addendum to this Agreement bearing the signatures of authorized officials of the Congregation and the Institute.

_____   _____
        For the Congregation   For the Institute

Appendix 2: Loans Make it Possible

From time to time inquiries are made whether the Concordia Historical Institute is interested in obtaining various historical materials on a loan basis. On other occasions the Institute may find it necessary to borrow certain resources from individuals and organizations for study, examination, identification, research, or display.

Whenever we are involved in arranging for loans, we are deeply concerned about preserving the integrity of the manuscripts, museum objects, pictures, and historical resources. We need to protect the rights of the owner of these resources as well as those of the Institute. Because of this, it is essential that a loan agreement identifying the conditions mutually acceptable between the lender/owner(s) and the Institute be identified. The attached "loan agreement" (Bulletin #15A) is designed for that purpose.

Loans may be arranged for a longer or shorter term. The specific termination date of the loan must be defined. Under certain conditions, a loan may also be arranged for on an indefinite period, but then provisions for renewal or release must be provided as well. Since such arrangements involve the establishment of legal ownership of the resources, it is extremely important that the owners and their successors be properly identified and their names and addresses retained on file at the Institute. The agreement must indicate the purpose and condition of such a loan and include specific references to the fact that the materials have been placed on loan 1) for examination; 2) for study; 3) for identification; 4) for an option to purchase; or 5) for display and exhibition purposes.

It is further imperative that the procedural routes for the termination or continuation of the loan be revealed. If any special obligations have been imposed on such a loan, these need to be indicated. Any questions or comments pertaining to the loan agreement should be brought to the Institute Director's attention. Thank you for giving this matter your consideration.

Reprinted from Aug. R. Suelflow, *Loans Make It Possible,* Department of Archives and History Bulletin 15 (St. Louis: Concordia Historical Institute, 1966).

LOAN AGREEMENT

Bulletin #15A
May 1966

CONCORDIA HISTORICAL INSTITUTE
Department of Archives and History
The Lutheran Church--Missouri Synod
801 DeMun Avenue
St. Louis, Missouri 63105

This Agreement, entered into the _____ day of _____, 19 _____, by and between Concordia Historical Institute (herein called "Institute") and:

Name: Name:
Address: Address:

Name: Name:
Address: Address:

(being herein referred to jointly as "Lender-Owners");

WITNESSETH: That

WHEREAS, Lender-Owners have delivered to the Institute at 801 DeMun Avenue, St. Louis, Missouri 63105, certain personal property (herein called "Objects"), described as, and to which have been assigned identifying file, serial, and/or other number(s)_____ to _____ (inclusive), as listed at the end of this agreement, and

WHEREAS, Lender-Owners desire to loan the described Objects to the Institute for the term provided herein;

NOW, THEREFORE, it is covenanted and agreed by and between the parties hereto as follows:

1. Supplemental lists of Objects attached hereto, which bear the signatures of the parties, are made a part of and subject to this Agreement.

2. Lender-Owners covenant that they are the sole owners of the Objects herein loaned, that no other person has any right, title, or interest in or to the same, that during the term of this loan or any renewal thereof the Lender-Owners will not sell or encumber said Objects or any interest therein, and Lender-Owners agree to indemnify the Institute against all loss, damage, expense, attorneys' fees, and/or penalty arising from any action on account of the alleged interest of any character whatsoever of any person in or to said Objects, irrespective of whether said Objects are in the possession of or under the custody and control of the Institute.

3. The possession of any Objects loaned to the Institute by Lender-Owners may be retained by the Institute for a term of six (6) months except as otherwise provided by addendum hereto.

4. The Lender-Owners may obtain upon the expiration of the term (or renewal thereof) for which said Objects are loaned, or within sixty (60) days thereafter, the return of said Objects, not theretofore returned to or abandoned by the Lender-Owners as provided herein, at the aforesaid offices of the Institute upon executing

a receipt for the same (by all the Lender-Owners), provided written demand for said Objects has been made upon the Institute by all the Lender-Owners at least thirty (30) days prior to the date upon which the return of said Objects is to be made. If the Lender-Owners desire to have said Objects returned to them at an address other than at the aforesaid offices of the Institute, all the Lender-Owners shall designate such address in the aforesaid written demand for said Objects. Upon receiving such written instructions from all the Lender-Owners, the Institute shall return said Objects to the Lender-Owners by depositing the same in the United States mails, addressed to such address as the Lender-Owners may designate, provided the Lender-Owners have theretofore executed and delivered a receipt for said Objects to the Institute, and deposited with the Institute such sum of money as the Institute shall deem necessary, to cover the cost of packing, shipping and in transit insurance.

5. The term for which said Objects are loaned may be renewed for a like or different term upon the execution of an addendum to this Agreement by the parties hereto. If the Lender-Owners fail to obtain the return of said Objects within sixty (60) days after the expiration of the term for which said Objects are loaned, the term of said loan shall be deemed to be renewed by the parties hereto for the same term as is originally provided herein.

6. The Institute may, at its discretion, return any or all Objects subject to this Agreement to the Lender-Owners at any time other than the expiration of the term (or renewal thereof) provided herein upon notifying the Lender-Owners of such intent by registered letter, addressed to the addresses of the Lender-Owners recorded in this Agreement, or to the last corrected addresses of which the Institute has been notified by the Lender-Owners. If such registered letter is acknowledged by one or more of the Lender-Owners, said Objects shall be delivered to said Lender-Owners who appear at the aforesaid offices of the Institute and execute a receipt for the same upon the date and at the time specified in said letter of notification. The Lender-Owners, if any, who do not so appear and execute a receipt for said Objects hereby consent to the delivery to and execution of a receipt by said Lender-Owners so appearing and executing such a receipt without liability of the Institute upon any ground whatsoever to said Lender-Owners. If such registered letter is not delivered to any of the Lender-Owners, or, if delivered, is not acknowledged by any of the Lender-Owners within thirty (30) days of the mailing of the same, or if delivered and acknowledged by any of said Lender-Owners but said Lender-Owners fail to execute a receipt for the same at the time and in the manner aforesaid, then in any of such events said Objects shall be deemed to have been abandoned by the Lender-Owners and all right, title, and interest in and to such Objects shall be deemed to have vested in the Institute with full authority to retain, dispose of, or deal in said Objects as the Institute's property without liability upon any ground whatsoever to the Lender-Owners.

7. The Lender-Owners may transfer ownership of said Objects to the Institute at any time upon the consent of the Institute.

8. The Institute shall not be required to insure Objects loaned to it by the Lender-Owners for any purpose. The Institute shall not be liable for the deterioration of or damage occurring to said Objects by reason of the normal aging process, useage, handling, acts of God and of nature, or for the safekeeping of said Objects beyond the exercise of such precautions as are now in force, or may hereafter be

put in force, for the safekeeping and preservation of the property of the Institute itself.

9.   The Institute shall not clean, repair, or restore Objects loaned to it by the Lender-Owners except in accordance with the written authorization of all the Lender-Owners.

10.   The Institute is authorized to mark said Objects with identification numbers, provided that reasonable care is exercised to apply marks that will not be injurious to said Objects.

11.   Plates, stamps, or other identification may be affixed to such Objects by the Lender-Owners indicating that they have been loaned in memory of an individual(s). The Institute does not, however, obligate itself to maintain such identification.

12.   The Institute agrees to abide by such limitations as to the use of said Objects as may be provided by addendum hereto.

13.   The Institute reserves the right to file, index, and catalog said Objects in its regular filing, indexing, and cataloging system. If separate filing, indexing, and cataloging of said Objects be maintained by the Institute, such files, indexes and catalogs may be nonetheless housed in conjunction with the general card catalog.

14.   While said Objects are in the possession and custody of the Institute they may be photographed, copied, or otherwise reproduced at the discretion of the Institute, whether or not for the profit of the Institute, provided, however, that authorization to photograph or otherwise copy said Objects for the profit of any person other than the Institute shall not be given by the Institute without written permission from all the Lender-Owners.

15.   The Lender-Owners agree to keep the Institute informed of any change in their permanent addresses, any change in the ownership of said Objects (whether by bequest, inheritance, or otherwise), and of any contemplated sale or loan of said Objects to any other person or institution upon the expiration of the term of this loan.

16.   This Agreement and the covenants herein contained, shall be binding upon the heirs, legatees, estates, guardians, and successors and assigns of the Lender-Owners. No modification or change in this Agreement may be made except by written addendum to this Agreement bearing the signatures of all the Lender-Owners and an authorized official of the Institute.

COMPLETE DESCRIPTION OF OBJECTS RECEIVED

MSS., unprinted documents	Author	Date	Pages	Condition
_____	_____	_____	_____	_____
_____	_____	_____	_____	_____
_____	_____	_____	_____	_____
_____	_____	_____	_____	_____

Books, pamphlets	Publisher			
_____	_____	_____	_____	_____
_____	_____	_____	_____	_____
_____	_____	_____	_____	_____
_____	_____	_____	_____	_____

Microfilm and photostats	Loc. of Orig.	Quantity
_____	_____	_____
_____	_____	_____

Museum Pieces	Historical Significance	Dimensions
_____	_____	_____
_____	_____	_____
_____	_____	_____
_____	_____	_____

(   ) Note here if description is continued on backside or on an additional page, due to lack of sufficient space above.

Special historical significance of the collection:_____

_____

_____

_____

_____

Use: ( )   Unrestricted, at the discretion of the Institute
       ( )   Restricted, to be used with permission of Institute Director only
       ( )   Sealed, not to be opened until _____

Ownership, in exceptional case should release and return of materials be requested:

       ( )   Lender retains exclusive rights to request return of materials
       ( )   Joint ownership (all co-owners must sign below)

Status: ( )   Permanent Loan
        ( )   Temporary Loan; expiration date:_____

CONCORDIA HISTORICAL INSTITUTE

By:_____
                        Director

Lender-Owners:

Name:_____

Address: _____

Name: _____

Address:_____

Name:_____

Address:_____

Name:_____

Address:_____

Appendix 3: Notes to Researchers

Welcome to the Historical Institute. One of our chief functions is to promote interest in the history of Lutheranism in America, particularly of The Lutheran Church — Missouri Synod, and to stimulate historical research. The collection is housed and serviced through the church budget. Researchers are encouraged to subscribe to our journal, the *Concordia Historical Institute Quarterly*. We are grateful for the opportunity to serve you.

General

A. The Institute is open for research Monday through Friday, 8:30 a.m. - 12:00 noon and 1:00 - 4:30 p.m. Our museum is also open on Saturday and Sunday afternoons from 2:00 - 5:00 p.m. However, because of our staff limitation, these latter periods are not the best in which to initiate research. If a program has been established prior to the weekend, arrangements can then be made to continue.

B. Members of the Institute may on occasion make arrangements with the Director to do research in the building in the evening or on Saturday morning. Such evening research may not extend beyond 10:00 p.m. These arrangements are subject to the availability of qualified Institute staff members to assist the researcher during such periods. As with weekend research, the research program must be established before evening arrangements are made.

C. A number of catalogues, card files and indexes are available. Not every individual item within the collection, of course, is catalogued. Among the general finding aids available are the following catalogues and inventories:
   1. Microfilm materials;
   2. Congregational histories;
   3. Manuscript collections; (Completion of such inventories is a high priority item for our staff. Completed inventories are available in the reference room.)
   4. Bibles, hymnals, catechisms and devotional literature;
   5. Biographical data;
   6. Foreign mission materials;
   7. Audio-visual resources;
   8. Museum objects;
   9. Union List of Lutheran Serials;
   10. Missouri Synod publications;
   11. C.F.W. Walther's writings.

D. For detailed, specific research, it is desirable to make advance arrangements with the Director. Reference assistance will be given by the staff wherever possible in finding relevant materials in a collection of more than 2,450,000 manuscripts and 56,500 books, pamphlets, periodicals and tracts.

E. Good service and housing are available near the Institute. Inquire for a list of motels and hotels. Guest rooms and food service may also be

Reprinted from Aug. R. Suelflow, *Notes to Researchers*, Department of Archives and History Bulletin 16 (St. Louis: Concordia Historical Institute, 1976).

available on the campus of Concordia Seminary where the Institute is located. Arrangements may be made directly with the Business Office, Concordia Seminary, 801 DeMun Ave., St. Louis, MO 63105.

F. The researcher is encouraged to make recommendations for the Institute's acquisition program.

Facilities

A. All researchers using materials from the Institute stacks must complete an "Application for Access to Resources." In signing this form the researcher accepts responsibility for materials made available for research and consents to a briefcase search if requested. Researchers unknown to us may also be asked to show two pieces of identification, one of which contains a picture.

B. The Institute operates with a "Closed Stack" system. All collections fit into one of the following access categories: 1) *Open* without restriction; 2) *Restricted* — access granted under certain conditions and with written permission of the donor; 3) *Sealed* — access denied to all until predetermined date. Generally, no researcher shall be granted access to any archives, manuscripts or private papers until 25 years have elapsed since their creation. Exceptions to this policy may be made upon special application to the Director in which the researcher demonstrates a need for the material and qualification to make use of it.

C. All research in the Institute building is normally conducted in the Polack Reference Room. The staff will make resources available in units of a usable size. The researcher is required to sign the "Stack Use Ledger" for all materials received from the stacks.

D. It is suggested that the researcher in his initial survey acquaint himself with all the potential resources available. Some of these may be used only on the premises and others can be checked out on loan. It is to his advantage, if limited in time, to utilize materials which are restricted to the building while in St. Louis, and to make arrangements for loans. The researcher should keep a careful record of all resources searched at the Institute in order that all possible sources for his project may be made available.

Services and Policies of Access

A. Transcripts, typescripts, manuscripts, photoduplicates, and/or rare sources may be read, quoted from and cited by qualified researchers, and may be reproduced for purposes of research. However, no reproductions, regardless of the instrument used, may be made without the expressed permission of the Institute. It is understood that copies made by the researcher, or provided by the Institute, are made exclusively as an aid to specific research. Prospective users should bear in mind the restrictions inherent in copyright law and in the common law, under which a writer or his heirs own the literary proper-

ty in his writings, including the right of first publication. It is the responsibility of the prospective user or his publisher to clear the rights or obtain the required permissions. Notes and xeroxing and briefcase must be presented to the attendant for inspection before the researcher leaves.

B. Photoduplication Services
1. Manuscript and archival materials may be reproduced if:
   a. The condition of the originals will permit.
   b. The originals have no gift, purchase, or legal restriction on reproduction. Written permission of the donor may be required to obtain copies of restricted material.
2. Photoduplication services are available at the Institute at a nominal cost. Xerox services may be obtained fairly quickly; photocopy and microfilm will require more time. In cases where large amounts of material are requested for reproduction, the Institute may prescribe a preferred method of copying and may provide for a reasonable time period in which to produce the copies.
3. Researchers may not file or deposit such reproductions in another depository without express permission. Further reproductions from such copies to the Institute after the research is completed.

C. Research and translation services are available for a fee. See the 'Summary of Service Charges' for specific costs.

D. Food, beverages and smoking are not permitted in the Reference Room. Typewriters, ball point pens, pencils and dictating equipment may be used. Fountain pens are prohibited. Please do not make notations of any sort on the resources used, or fold anew, trace or manhandle materials. The researcher will be held responsible where evidence of destruction or deterioration due to mishandling is apparent. We reserve the right to refuse use of our collection to those who violate the rules.

E. Keep unbound papers in the order in which they are delivered. You are encouraged to notify the attendant of any manuscript apparently misfiled.

F. Full and complete credit shall be given to the Institute when its resources have been extensively used, both in the foreword and in the individual footnote citations. In some cases, proper credit shall also be given to the original donor or the person interviewed in the case of an oral history source. We would appreciate notification when a published work results from use of our collection.

G. When certain confidential and restricted resources are used, the Institute reserves the right to read the manuscript produced and prohibit the use of direct quotations from such resources.

Good hunting. We sincerely hope that you will enjoy your research and that we may have the privilege of your frequent return. Your suggestions for improvement of our services are always welcome.

APPLICATION FOR ACCESS TO RESOURCES

Bulletin #16
October 1976

Date: _____

I have read Bulletin #16. I hereby apply for access to the resources
of the Institute and agree to comply with the conditions and policies established to govern the use of its records. I agree that I am responsible
for all materials made available to me, and I agree to a briefcase check
if requested.

Signature: _____

1. Name: _____

    Address: _____

    _____

2. TOPIC OF RESEARCH: _____
    a. Related topics (cross references, details, resources needed):
    _____
    _____
    b. Purpose of research: _____
    c. If thesis or dissertation, indicate institution and advisor:
    _____
    d. Is publication contemplated? _____
    e. Have you corresponded with the Institute about this? _____
3. Name of institution or organization of affiliation, occupation:
    _____
4. REFERENCES (Give names and addresses of two persons who are
    qualified to recommend you as a reputable researcher):
    _____
    _____
    _____
5. Are you a member of the Institute? _____ While membership is not
    required to make use of our research facilities and resources, we en-
    courage you to consider this as a way both to benefit personally from
    reading the Institute QUARTERLY and other materials and to assist us
    in continuing to offer our services to you and others.

- -

6. STAFF APPROVAL: _____ a. Limited to Historical Library

                    _____ b. Archives and Manuscripts

                    _____ c. Stack Privileges

    Approval granted by: _____

SPECIAL APPLICATION
FOR ACCESS TO RESOURCES
OF A RESTRICTED NATURE

Bulletin 16B   Date: _____
February 1976

Generally, no researcher shall be granted access to any archives,
manuscripts or private papers until 25 years have elapsed since
their creation. Exceptions to this policy may be made by the
Director when the researcher is especially qualified to examine
such records, or when the welfare of the church demands such
access.

    I have read Bulletin 16 and have previously filed
    Bulletin 16A, Application for Access to Resources, which
    has been approved. I hereby apply to the Institute
    Director for access to materials which have been
    created within the past 25 years, and I agree to comply
    with the conditions and policies of the Institute
    governing use of these materials.

                              Signature:_____

1. Name (Please Print): _____

2. Topic: _____

3. Materials requested: _____

    _____

    _____

4. Please explain the need for access to these restricted
   materials in terms of your research project:

----

5. Access approved:_____Date_____
                        Director
6. Dates materials used:_____

7. Staff member assisting researcher:_____

NOTES